A COVER FOR GLORY

A COVER *for* GLORY

A Biblical Defense
for Headcoverings

DALE PARTRIDGE

Relearn Press
PRESCOTT, ARIZONA

© 2023 by Relearn.org. All rights reserved.

No portion of this book may be reproduced, stored in a retrieval system, or transmitted in any form or by any means— electronic, mechanical, photocopy, recording, scanning, or other—except for brief quotations in critical reviews or articles, without the prior written permission of the publisher.

Published in Prescott, Arizona by Relearn.org
Written by Dale Partridge
First Edition / First Printing
Cover Image: Painting: "Young Woman Praying in Church" (1854) by Jules Breton.
Printed in the U.S.A.

Scripture quotations taken from the (NASB®) New American Standard Bible®, Copyright © 1960, 1971, 1977, 1995, 2020 by The Lockman Foundation. Used by permission. All rights reserved. lockman.org.

Relearn Press is the publishing division of
Relearn.org. For information, please contact us through our website at Relearn.org.

To my wife, Veronica, who is an emblem of biblical femininity in our home. You are a virtuous woman, nurturing our family with love, wisdom, and steadfast devotion, a true embodiment of a godly woman.

Our Ministry

The mission of Relearn.org is simple:
To bring the church back to the Bible.
This is the driving force behind each of our
books, digital products, and podcasts.

Our Companion Ministries

MailTheGospel.org
ReformationSeminary.com
StandInVictory.org
UltimateMarriage.com
KingsWayBible.org

Table *of* Contents

Foreword by Joel Webbon
Setting Expectations

SECTION ONE

01: Looking Strange for God — 09

02: A Short History of Headcoverings — 19

03: Feminism and the Falling Away of Headcoverings — 41

SECTION TWO

04: Building Confidence with Context — 49

05: 11:2 A Praise for Obedience — 55

06: 11:3–6 An Argument from Authority — 65

07: 11:7–9 An Argument from Creation — 85

08: 11:10 An Argument from the Spiritual Realm — 121

09: 11:11–12 Men and Women Equal Before God — 129

10: 11:13–15 An Argument from Nature	135
11: 11:16 An Argument from the Church	151

SECTION THREE

Chapter #12: Conclusion	157
Important Questions, Quick Answers	169

CLOSING MATTERS

Appendix B: Block Diagram of 1 Cor. 11:2–16	179
Special Thanks	187
Bibliography	191

Foreword

UNCOVERING THE TRUTH ABOUT HEADCOVERINGS

UNCOVERING THE TRUTH
ABOUT HEADCOVERINGS
By Joel Webbon

Whenever we see 1900 years of Church History (95%) universally dominated by a particular practice, we should take serious pause. Although we are often inclined to overcomplicate certain doctrinal matters, the simple truth is that there can only be two valid explanations that make sense of the Church's very recent change regarding its position

Explanation One
For 1900 years, the Church universally believed women should cover their heads in worship because there were virtually no able theologians and pastors available to properly exegete the Scripture on this matter. Only in the last century has God finally provided his Church with competent theologians and pastors equipped with the necessary exegetical prowess for rightly interpreting 1 Corinthians 11.

Explanation Two

Over the past century, Western Civilization has been uniquely marked by an exponentially high degree of Feminism, far greater than at any other time in human history. This unparalleled dominance of Feminism has quickly crept into every facet of our society, including the Church, causing theologians and pastors to complicate what virtually every Christian before them saw as simple.

Now, be honest. Which explanation do you think is more probable? Should we say that the Twentieth Century is uniquely set apart from the rest of human history because of its superior theologians? Or is it more reasonable to say that the Twentieth Century is uniquely set apart from the rest of human history due to its unparalleled embrace of Modern Feminism?

Of course, some readers will insist that I am oversimplifying the matter. So allow me to address the issue from another angle by paraphrasing what the late, great R. C. Sproul once said on this subject:

"All I know is this—There *might* be a commandment in Scripture that requires a woman to cover her head in worship, but there is certainly *not* a commandment in Scripture that forbids a woman from covering her head in worship. Therefore, the woman who covers her head is merely taking the safer, and more logical, position."

The vast majority of God's commandments are not complicated, but they're still hard to obey. It's been said that obedience to Christ is like chopping wood. Chopping wood is not rocket science. It doesn't require a Ph.D. Likewise, a woman's submission to the Bible's command to cover her head in worship does not require that she be an expert theologian. Instead, it requires that she be willing to resist the fear of man.

In light of all this, it is quite possible that Dale Partridge has provided for us the single most persuasive, comprehensive, and concise argument for a woman covering her head in worship. And yet, my suspicion is that the vast majority of today's Christians are hindered in their obedience to this specific command, not because 1 Corinthians 11 is particularly difficult to understand, but because the Evangelical Church in the West is so compromised in the area of Feminism, a woman's willingness to take a visible and public stand will likely cost her dearly.

So I conclude this foreword with a strong exhortation to the reader:

Partridge's work on this subject is so profound and compelling that virtually every Christian who reads this book will find their conscience thoroughly inspired in such a way that they can no longer dismiss this discussion without serious consideration and prayer. Dale leads with Scripture and allows the text to talk. Therefore, prepare yourself for earnest introspection and wade into these waters with a heart, mind, and soul that is receptive to this critical doctrine on headcoverings.

Joel Webbon
March 2023
President, Right Response Ministries

SETTING EXPECTATIONS

This book is written to be defensive and persuasive. At the core, it is a verse-by-verse commentary on 1 Corinthians 11:2–16. In Section One, I will offer you my own personal experience with headcoverings, a brief history of the doctrine, and the context for the passage. In Section Two, I have broken up the passage into seven segments where I will offer my commentary, explain the meaning, defend the meaning, apply the meaning, and move on. In Section Three, I offer my conclusion and answer a variety of common questions. Ultimately, my hope is to provide you with a compelling argument, backed by Scripture, for the practice of headcoverings.

Section One

A DEFENSE FROM TESTIMONY AND HISTORY

Chapter 01

LOOKING STRANGE FOR GOD

In 2014, I was working through the text of 1 Corinthians 11:2–16 on the matter of headcoverings. My wife, Veronica, and I came from a large non-denominational church in Southern California, and, outside of our time visiting the Amish and Mennonite communities of Pennsylvania, we had never heard of or seen a woman wearing a headcovering.

However, after spending several weeks carefully expositing the text and having significant conversations, we both concluded that headcoverings were not merely limited to the local customs of the Corinthian era but were a universal Christian practice for today and all time.

Interestingly, for my wife, the hardest part of obeying this command was not that Scripture had called her to symbolize the doctrine of headship. The hardest part for her was wearing something on her head at church. In a time when headcoverings were virtually non-existent in the Western Church, she didn't want to appear unusual, awkward, or legalistic. Furthermore, as an introvert, she had zero interest in drawing attention to herself. She imagined her new conviction would draw as much attention to herself as walking into a dark room with a floodlight strapped to her head. However, I reminded her that being a physical example of holiness should never cause her shame, but honor. If her obedience causes a scene—praise God!

That following Sunday, we walked into our church, sat down among our friends, and, as worship commenced, Veronica reached into her bag, grabbed a beautifully laced headcovering the size of a large bandana, and tied it around her hair. I know this took a good deal of courage from her. However, this was only possible because her fear of the Lord far outpaced her fear of looking strange.

Veronica was operating from a place of biblical conviction and clarity. That is, she understood the passage of Scripture she was obeying. She grasped the theological and doctrinal depths of this command, and, as a result, she was committed to carrying out her duty despite her fears. I share this because the heart cannot obey what the mind does not understand. Sure, we can always obey blindly but, heart driven obedience cannot come from mental ignorance. Jesus tells us that the greatest commandment is to "Love the Lord your God with all your heart, with all your soul, and with all your *mind*." That is, intellectual comprehension is a vital piece of sincere obedience.

It's for that reason I have decided to write this short book. To carefully exposit this passage on headcoverings and offer men and women an accessible and straightforward teaching on this important Christian doctrine.

Diminishing the Doctrine

Some opponents of headcoverings attempt to diminish the importance of this doctrine by saying, "It's not a salvation issue." That's true, but neither is church government, baptism, or eschatology and yet we are certainly concerned about those matters. Other opponents argue by saying that headcoverings are only mentioned once in Scripture and, therefore, are an unfounded doctrine. However, there are several commands in Scripture that only appear once. For example, 1 Timothy 5:8 is the only passage in Scripture that directly teaches Christian men to provide for their families. Should we ignore the jurisdiction of this passage because of its low frequency? Certainly not. The reality is, while this passage on headcoverings is found only once, the principle is painted across the Scriptures. In addition, it's not one short verse from Scripture but fifteen verses on the matter. That is, there are more verses in the New Testament dedicated to headcoverings than there are to church membership, church attendance, parenting, and even the inerrancy of Scripture.

Furthermore, when someone argues against a doctrine by its low frequency of appearance, they diminish both the authority of the Scriptures and the biblical author. For example, Jesus never spoke directly about deacons in the church; does this diminish Paul's teaching? No. To object to a particular doctrine simply because it does not appear in several places in the Bible makes frequency the determining factor of what passages of Scripture are authoritative. This is a poor application of hermeneutics (principles of interpretation). Sound interpretation requires us to know there are portions of Scripture that are *descriptive* but not *prescriptive*. There are local customs and universal commands. There are literary genres, symbolism, and figures of speech. There is grammar, history, audience, and context. Ultimately, *how* we interpret Scripture *really* matters. We will discuss this more in later chapters. But for now, we can have confidence that God has chosen to include this passage on headcoverings in our Bible for our edification and for His glory.

Lastly, when it comes to headcoverings, there is a right and wrong view here. In other words, someone will be wrong. If headcoverings are biblical and binding, as I will argue, then those who omit obedience to this command are sinning, even if by ignorance. However, if headcoverings are not binding for today, then those who commit themselves to this practice are not in sin but merely honoring their own conscience. That is to say, the party of omission of obedience holds greater risk before God. Therefore, do not rush through this book. Consider the content, be prayerful in moments of uncertainty, and be patient as the Word of God penetrates your heart and mind.

Gender Distinctions in an Amalgamated Culture

We are living in a time plagued with confusion regarding gender identity and male and female roles. We are lacking concrete definitions for what it means to be a man or a woman. Gender distinctions are being ruthlessly removed, stores are eliminating gender-specific toy sections, clothing has become androgynous or unisex, movies are promoting masculine females and effeminate men, and any sign or symbol that represents biblical definitions of gender is being destroyed, canceled, or mocked.

Furthermore, authors, social activists, celebrities, and academics have taken to various forms of media to publish works attempting to bring about their own views and theories on the matter. However, when it comes to gender and their associated roles, the Bible alone has the answers. Humanity will not find what it's looking for by looking within itself; we must look solely to the Scriptures to find these answers.

You might wonder, "How does gender confusion connect to the practice of headcoverings?" As you will see in this book, we serve a God who designs, who orders, and who makes promises to His people. What's more, we serve a God who graciously gives His people physical signs, visual symbols, and spiritual seals to help them remember those designs, orders, and promises.

In the Old Testament, God did this with the rainbow, sacrificial blood, the solar system, clothing, and even food. In the New Testament, water, bread and wine, and marriage act as visual pictures of spiritual truths. In other words, God knows that humans have finite minds, and we need the power of symbolism to gain and retain understanding of divine truth. That is, we need visual queues and earthly patterns to reiterate His structure and His ways. The doctrine of headcoverings falls squarely into this category.

Headcoverings are God's New Testament practice to

symbolize gender distinctions among His people and the world. It is logical to believe that when biblical symbols disappear from society, what those symbols represent will eventually be forgotten. For that reason, I don't believe it's a coincidence that when headcoverings disappeared from the church around the 1960s, that confusion around gender began to scale. Ultimately, when you remove visual reminders of the truth, the truth will soon be forgotten, too.

The lie is to believe that if we don't adopt headcoverings as the biblical symbol for gender distinctions, then we will be left with no symbols at all, but that is not the case. The culture will always provide its own symbols, and they will tell their own stories that war against the truth. This is why you can look at a person, in some cases, and know their sexual orientation or their political party. A symbol-less society cannot exist. It is not *if* you will symbolize with your outward appearance but *how* and *what* you will symbolize. Therefore, my argument in this book is that God has provided Christian men and women a way to symbolize their masculinity and femininity that is biblical, orderly, powerful, and radiates rich theological truth to an onlooking world.

However, the solution to today's gender mess is not merely requiring millions of religious women to put scarves on their heads. No, outward modification will never make a lasting change. This was the very problem of the past and why headcoverings, which were practiced for nearly 2,000 years, suddenly disappeared. They became symbols without meaning. They were a practice that had no substance. That was never God's will for this beautiful doctrine.

Like any command of Scripture, the doctrine of headcoverings must be obeyed from the heart. That is, the generational sticking power of any biblical truth is when the motive for obedience stems from the love of God in Christ combined with theological understanding. Without these two driving forces of heart and mind, you will have women covering their heads, but not for long.

Ultimately, looking strange is nothing new for God's children. According to Scripture, we are a peculiar people, set apart from the ways of the world, and called to live lives that cause curiosity and produce conversations (1 Pet. 2:9 KJV; 3:15–16). Therefore, covering your head during spiritual functions to symbolize your authority in God's created order may be provocative to the world, but it's normal to God. In the end, peculiar practices like these give the world a glimpse into the counterintuitive economy of the Kingdom of God.

The Purpose of the Pages Ahead

I wrote this book because I wish I had a clear and accessible resource like this when I was wrestling through this passage years ago. My hope is that you will see that this doctrine, while it may be difficult put into practice, is not all that difficult to understand. You will have questions, and you will face challenging truths, but I am convinced that if you approach this passage with a humble heart, this journey of discovery will be an immense blessing. So together, we will walk through 1 Corinthians 11:2–16, verse by verse.

But before we get started, let's look behind us for a moment. The historical context for headcoverings in the Church is considerable. Years ago, a fellow pastor was working through this doctrine and was compelled by another brother who sent him this:

> "Here's a little historical fact; make of it what you will. In every single denomination of Christianity on every continent, Roman Catholic, Coptic, Eastern Orthodox, Lutheran, Continental Reformed, Anabaptist, Anglican, Presbyterian, Puritan, Congregational, Separatists, General Baptists, Particular Baptists, Southern Baptists, American Baptists, Methodists, Restoration Movement, Amish, Mennonite, and Pentecostal women wore headcoverings until the 1900s."[1]

In other words, his friend showed him what I'm about to show you—headcoverings are overwhelmingly historical. That is to say, this next chapter will be compelling but do not allow its contents alone to convince you. Reserve your persuasion for Section Two, where I will exposit the passage itself. Simply put, I do not want your beliefs anchored in history, but in Scripture. When Scripture is your foundation, you will not be shaken. But

---

1 Brian Sauvé, Lexy Sauvé. 2023. Bright Hearth: What About Head Coverings? New Christendom Press. https://podcasts.apple.com/us/podcast/what-about-head-coverings/id1616730798?i=1000599283561.

when history, philosophy, or religious traditions are your root, you will be easily knocked down.

Chapter 02

A SHORT HISTORY OF HEADCOVERINGS

As Christians, it is vital that we understand our place in church history. We have all been uniquely placed into the timeline of God's covenant people in this age.

To not grasp the Kingdom development accomplished before us would be forfeiting a great wealth of wisdom for our Christian life. Any person who willfully remains unfamiliar with history is like a leaf that doesn't know it is part of a tree.[1]

The value of church history is not foreign to the Scriptures. In Romans 15:4, Paul affirms the leveraging of church history when he says, "For whatever was written in former days was written for our instruction, that through endurance and through the encouragement of the Scriptures we might have hope." 1 Corinthians 10:11 also says, "Now all these things happened to them as examples, and they were written for our admonition, upon whom the ends of the ages have come." Namely, the Scriptures themselves emphasize the importance of learning from

---

1 Michael Crichton, n.d. "Michael Crichton Quotes." Goodreads.com. Accessed February 23, 2023. https://www.goodreads.com/quotes/188569-if-you-don-t-know-history-then-you-don-t-know-anything.

past events and experiences as a way to guide and inform our worship in the present.

Too many Christians are, as C.S. Lewis says, "chronological snobs" who only value the opinions of men from the era in which they live. However, the Bible uses the word "remember" 164 times and paints a concern for the past among God's people.[2] That is to say, this generation of the church cannot forget the overwhelming archive of writings and resources by other Holy Spirit-filled believers from our past. Charles Spurgeon once said, "It seems odd that certain men who talk so much of what the Holy Spirit reveals to themselves should think so little of what he has revealed to others."[3]

Therefore, let us look to the history of headcoverings to see how the saints before us interpreted and applied this passage of Scripture.

The Old Testament Church Era (c. 5000 B.C.–70 A.D.)

As we traverse the vast expanse of history, we begin with the Old Testament Church Era, spanning from around 5000 B.C. to 70 A.D. While covering (or veiling) of women has a rich cultural history, there is no historical evidence that headcoverings were given any theological or spiritual significance until Paul's teaching in 1 Corinthians 11. In ancient cultures, headcovering

---

[2] I drew inspiration from this helpful article: Boekestein, William. n.d. "Six Benefits of Studying Church History." Reformation 21. Accessed February 2023. https://www.reformation21.org/blog/six-benefits-of-studying-church-history.

[3] Charles H Spurgeon. 2022. Commenting & Commentaries. Legare Street Press.

was for geographic function, fashion, or, in some cases, modesty. In the Old Testament, however, we only see two women cover themselves.

The first is Rebekah in Genesis 24:64–65, "And Rebekah lifted up her eyes, and when she saw Isaac, she dismounted from the camel and said to the servant, "Who is that man, walking in the field to meet us?" The servant said, "It is my master." So she took her veil and covered herself." The second instance is in Genesis 38:15, where Tamar disguises herself as a prostitute by covering her face.

Interestingly, these two instances are carried out by a virgin (Rebekah) and a harlot (Tamar), making it difficult to determine the purpose of ancient veiling. However, Numbers 5:18 discusses the punishment of a woman for harlotry was to present her before the Tabernacle of the Lord "and uncover the woman's head" as a sign of shame. John Gill, the respected Bible commentator and predecessor of Charles Spurgeon, wrote on this verse, "Uncover the woman's head; not her face, but the covering of her head, the hairs of which were wrapped up in a cloth, and this was done that she might appear with the greater shame and confusion, and as one that was found guilty and condemned; and that she might be seen by all, and others might be deterred from committing the like sin; and that it might be known she was dealt with not as a wife, but as a harlot."[4]

---

4 John Gill, Exposition of the Old and New Testaments, vol. 1 (London: Mathews and Leigh, 1809), Numbers 5:18, accessed from "StudyLight.org," https://www.studylight.org/commentaries/geb/numbers-5.html.

Therefore, there is clear evidence that Hebrew women covered their heads as an act of feminine modesty but, at this time, there was no explicit biblical command to do so.

During the Archaic and Hellenistic periods, Greek men and women wore what was called a *himitation* which was a mantle or wrap used to cover the head and shoulder that was exposed from the chiton (an ancient Greco-Roman garb).[5]

Generally speaking, the custom of this era was that married women covered and unmarried women did not. Caroline Galt, who wrote Veiled Ladies, published her research in the American Journal of Archaeology in 1931. She quoted a document from 1500 B.C. that states, "If she goes out into the street during the day, she is to veil herself. The captive (married) woman who, without the mistress (a female servant), goes out in the street is to be veiled. The hierodule (slave) who is married to a man is to be veiled in the street. The one who is not married to a man is to have her head uncovered in the street and is not to veil herself. The harlot is not to veil herself; her head is to be uncovered."[6]

As it pertains to worship, within Greek culture, both men and women engaged in worship with their heads uncovered, while in Roman culture, both sexes practiced worship with their heads covered.[7] The Latin epic poem *The Aeneid* written by Virgil

---

[5] Caroline M. Galt. "Veiled Ladies." *American Journal of Archaeology* 35, no. 4 (1931): 373–93. https://doi.org/10.2307/498098.

[6] Caroline M. Galt. "Veiled Ladies."

[7] H. T. Peck, (ed.), *Harper's Dictionary of Classical Literature and Antiquities* (London: Osgood, 1897 [1896]), pp. 676, 1670.

between 29 and 19 B.C., says, "And our heads are shrouded before the altar with a Phrygian vestment."[8] This covering of men during worship is also confirmed by several ancient structures, such as Trajan's Column, which still stands today.

Headcoverings undoubtedly possess a diverse and vibrant cross-cultural heritage. However, the crucial aspect to emphasize is that no culture previously distinguished between men uncovering their heads and women covering their heads during worship. This distinction implies that the practice set forth in 1 Corinthians 11:2–16 was a novel and exclusive practice of the Christian faith.

The Early Church (c. 70–215 A.D.)

This period is considered the cultural birth of Christendom. Marked by significant growth and development, despite facing numerous challenges, Christianity continued to spread throughout the Roman Empire. This time was saturated with both internal and external conflicts, including persecution and theological debates. But it was this era that laid the groundwork for the Church's expansion and establishment in the centuries to follow.

As the early church fathers began writing theology, commentaries, and epistles to the church, we began to see a unified practice and instruction regarding headcoverings. Clement of Alexandria, in writing about the appropriate dress for corporate worship, says, "Woman and man are to go to church

---

[8] Virgil, Aeneid, iii., 545.

decently attired, with natural step, embracing silence, possessing unfeigned love, pure in body, pure in heart, fit to pray to God. Let the woman observe this further.... For this is the wish of the Word, since it is becoming for her to pray veiled."[9] In another writing referencing 1 Corinthians 11:10, he writes, "Because of the angels ... let her be veiled."[10]

In the second century, the great theologian Tertullian of Carthage said, "The Christian man ... [is] under no obligation to wear a covering," and the woman's head "is bound to have the veil."[11] And in speaking of those women who did not cover or only partially covered themselves during worship, he writes, "How severe a chastisement will they likewise deserve who during the psalms and at any mention of God remain uncovered."[12] He goes on to gently ridicule those women who lack proper coverage, jesting their insufficient attire, "Even when about to spend time in prayer itself, with the utmost readiness, they place a fringe, tuft, or any thread whatever on the crowns of their heads, and suppose

---

9 Phillip Schaff. 2017. Ante-Nicene Fathers: Volume II. Fathers of the Second Century: Tatian, Theophilus of Antioch, Athenagoras of Athens, Clement of Alexandria. Two, Book Five, The Instructor, Book 3, Chapter 11. Edited by Alexander Roberts and James Donaldson. Grand Rapids, MI: Christian Classics Ethereal Library). 469.

10 Clement of Alexandria. 2005. "The Instructor. Book III Chapter XI." Early Christian Writings. 2005. http://www.earlychristianwritings.com/text/clement-instructor-book3.html.

11 Phillip Schaff. Ante-Nicene Fathers, Volume 3. Grand Rapids, MI: Christian Classics Ethereal Library.

12 Tertullian. "On the Veiling of Virgins: Chapter 1. Truth Rather to Be Appealed to Than Custom, and Truth Progressive in Its Developments." New Advent. https://www.newadvent.org/fathers/0403.htm.

themselves to be covered."[13]

John Chrysostom, who is known as one of the great theologians of the early church, also speaks to headcoverings. One of his most extensive exegetical works is that of 1 Corinthians. He writes to the women in regard to the passage on headcoverings, "Neither do thou ... not being covered ... pray before God, lest thou insult both thyself and Him that hath honored thee." He then argues against a woman's hair being a sufficient covering by instructing women to add a physical cloth that "not nature only, but also her own will may have a part in her acknowledgment of subjection."[14]

Interestingly, during my research, I spent several hours searching for theologians between the first and fourth centuries who came to a different conclusion concerning the doctrine and practice of headcoverings. Honestly, I could not find one. By the end of the fourth century, the *Apostolic Constitutions*, which is a robust collection of early Christian literature, records that when the church was gathered and especially during the time of communion, women had "their heads covered, as is becoming the order of women."[15] The word "becoming" does not mean a new development but what was the "appropriate" order of women. For

---

13 Alexander Roberts, ed. 2007. The Ante-Nicene Fathers: The Writings of the Fathers down to A.d. 325 Volume IV Fathers of the Third Century -Tertullian Part 4; Minucius Felix. New York, NY: Cosimo Classics. 469.

14 John Chrysostom. 2012. The Homilies of S. John Chrysostom, Archbishop of Constantinople on the First Epistle of St. Paul the Apostle to the Corinthians. Homily 26 on 1 Corinthians 11:2–16. General Books.

15 Ernest Cushing Richardson, Bernhard Pick, and James Donaldson. 2015. The Ante-Nicene Fathers. Translations of the Writings of the Fathers down to A.d. 325 Volume 7, Book II, Section VII, On Assembling in the Church. Arkose Press.

example, it is becoming of a woman to not dress immodestly, but to demonstrate prudence in her appearance.

The great Bible translator Jerome, who was the first to transcribe the entire Bible into Latin, said that in places of worship, women must "not ... go about with heads uncovered in defiance of the Apostle's command."[16] Augustine, who is arguably the most significant theologian for the first 1500 years of the Church said of headcoverings, "It is not becoming ... to uncover their hair since the Apostle commands women to keep their heads covered."[17] In his essay "Of the Work of Monks," which critiques the idleness prevalent within the monastic community, he passionately disputes the idea that hair serves as a sufficient covering.[18]

This theme continues in the writings of Hippolytus, Ambrose of Milan, Severian of Gabala, Basil of Cesarea, and Theodoret of Cyrus. In addition to these early church Fathers, there are the written canons with explicit affirmations of the practice of headcoverings. They are dated from the third to fifth century: *Apostolic Church Order*, *Apostolic Constitutions*, *Didascalia Apostolorum*, and *Testamentum Domini*. For further study, you can find all of these statements and more in R. Gryson's book, *The Ministry of Women in the Early Church*.

---

16 Philip Schaff, ed. 2007. Nicene and Post-Nicene Fathers: Second Series, Volume VI Jerome: Letters and Select Works. New York, NY: Cosimo Classics.

17 Sister Wilfrid Parsons. 1956. Letters, Volume 5 (204–270) (The Fathers of the Church, Volume 32). Catholic University of America Press.

18 Philip Schaff. (1887) 2012. Nicene and Post-Nicene Fathers. Vol. 3. Buffalo, NY: Christian Literature Publishing Co.

Another convincing piece of evidence is the widespread use of art for historical record-keeping. Various media, such as paintings, carvings, sculptures, stone inscriptions, and wall art, were employed for this purpose. Ancient Rome hosted miles of catacombs (underground or subterranean burial grounds). These were of Jewish origin, but by the first century, Christians had over 60 known catacombs that made up over 500 acres of underground galleries and burial sites. Throughout these ancient illustrations, we see a consistent theme of Christian women worshiping with a headcovering.[19]

In conclusion, the early church consistently emphasized the importance of headcoverings for women in worship. Their theological writings, biblical commentaries, and various art forms serve as the historical evidence that headcoverings were considered an integral and appropriate part of women's attire during worship.

The Middle Ages (C. 450–1500 A.D.)

As the Middle Ages commenced, the Christian Church embraced greater formality through councils, addressing various issues, including the use of headcoverings. In the Synod of Auxere (585 A.D.) in France, we see that women are to remain veiled during the Lord's Supper and the Synod of Rome, which stated,

---

19 Renee Ellison. 2022. The Biblical Headcovering: Scarf of Hidden Power. Arizona: Independent Publishing.; cf. A. T. Robertson, Word Pictures in the New Testament, Vol. IV (Nashville: Broadman Press, 1931), 162; Alexandra Croom, Roman Clothing and Fashion (Tempus Publishing, 2000), 80; The Online Bridgeman Art Library.

"Woman praying in church without her head covered brings shame upon her head, according to the word of the Apostle."[20] At the Council of Liège (1287 A.D.), we see that members of the clergy (men) are not permitted to cover their heads in church.[21]

The famous Roman Catholic theologian Thomas Aquinas (c. 1250 A.D.) shows his support in his commentary on 1 Corinthians that states, "It pertains to a man's dignity ... not to wear a covering on his head ... to show that he is immediately subject to God; but the woman should wear a covering to show that besides God she is naturally subject to another."[22] The French Bishop Guillaume Durand, in speaking about proper behavior in the church, writes, "A woman must cover her head in the church."[23]

Heinrich Von Langenstein was a German theologian (c.1325–1397 A.D.) who wrote a small teaching that included instruction regarding the use of headcoverings that said, "The woman wears a headdress so that it may be recognized that she

---

[20] Alvin J. Schmidt, ed. 1880. The Liturgy and Ritual of the Celtic Church. Vol. 10. The Church Quarterly Review. Cf., Veiled and Silenced (Mercer University Press, 1989), 136. Mansi, Giovan Domenico, Philippe Labbe, and Jean Baptiste Martin. 2019. Sacrorum Conciliorum Nova Et Amplissima Collectio, Cujus Johannes Dominicus Mansi Et Post Ipsius Mortem Florentius Et Venetianus Editores AB Anno 1758 Ad Annum 1798 Priores Triginta Unum Tomos Ediderunt, Nunc Autem Continuatat Et Absoluta, Volume 33. Wentworth Press.

[21] Gabriela Signori. 2005. Reflections on an Asymmetrical Relationship in The Medieval History Journal. London : Sage Publications.

[22] Thomas Acquinas. 2012. Commentary on the Letters of Saint Paul to the Corinthians (Latin-English Edition). Edited by The Aquinas Institute. Translated by Fabian R. Larcher. Aquinas Institute.

[23] Gulielmus Durandus. 2008. The Rationale Divinorum Officiorum: The Foundational Symbolism of the Early Church, Its Structure, Decoration, Sacraments, and Vestments. Louisville, KY: Fons Vitae.

is subordinate to the man."[24]

Interestingly, this era has very little content on headcoverings, but not without good reason. First, when church councils make formal statements on a particular matter, less supplemental teaching is needed. Second, when a practice is so culturally ingrained in a generation, teaching its observance becomes less necessary. For example, there is no volume of material in this era teaching against homosexuality. Why? Because it was not a significant issue facing the church. At this point in history, headcoverings were the ordinary means of Christian conduct.

The Reformation To the Present (c. 1500–Present A.D.)

If there was any time in church history that was marked by an extravagant commitment to the faithful interpretation and application of Scripture, it was during the Protestant Reformation. The word "Protestant" came from the word protest and was an era characterized by challenging the Roman Catholic view that Christian doctrine and practice were defined by the Pope, church tradition, and Scripture. This tri-fold commitment led to the perversion of the Gospel, among other important matters. As a result, the defining ethic birthed out of the Reformation was *Sola Scriptura* which is the principle that *Scripture alone* had the authority to define Christian doctrine and practice.

Thanks to the Gutenberg Press, for the first time in church history, thousands of Christians could own and read a Bible in

---

[24] Roberta Milliken, ed. A Cultural History of Hair in the Middle Ages. United Kingdom, Bloomsbury Publishing, 2020, Pg. 163.

their own language. In addition, theological discourse, commentaries, treatises, and printed sermons exploded in popularity. The consequence was rapid growth in biblical and theological literacy. If headcoverings were simply the religious tradition of a biblically illiterate generation and the doctrine had no real biblical footing, then this generation of Reformers would have eliminated the practice. However, that is exactly the opposite of what happened.

The very men who were responsible for bringing the church back to the Bible were also the greatest proponents of this doctrine on headcoverings. Men like Martin Luther, Hugh Latimer, John Calvin, John Knox, John Bunyan, and scores of others. These men came at the end of the scholastic era, which was a movement characterized by a renewed emphasis on systematic learning, logic, and critical reasoning. Namely, these men were raised in an era of rich theological study becoming scholars capable of interpreting the Scriptures in Hebrew, Aramaic, Greek, and Latin. They were men ready to give up their lives for their commitment to *Sola Scriptura*, and some did. For that generation of Christians, the idea of adopting practices without a clear biblical basis or embracing careless interpretations was quite uncommon.

Below, I have compiled a brief list of scholars and theologians from the Reformation to the present who have affirmed the doctrine of headcoverings.

In a historical study of Martin Luther's view of women, Susan Karant-Nunn records Luther stating, "The wife ... shall not rule over her husband, but be subject and obedient to him. For that reason, the wife wears a headdress, that is, the veil on her head."[25] In addition, and more specifically, Luther did directly affirm the doctrine of headcoverings as stated in 1 Corinthians 11:2–16 when he said, "Because of this, the wife has not been created out of the head, so that she shall not rule over her husband, but be subject and obedient to him. For that reason, the wife wears a headdress, that is, the veil on her head, as St. Paul writes in 1 Corinthians." He continues to say, "Fur and head coverings are women's most attractive and honorable and most genuine and most necessary adornment."[26]

Bishop Hugh Latimer, who was one of the Oxford Martyrs and burned alive under the reign of Bloody Mary in 1555, once said of this passage on headcoverings, "Paul saith that 'a woman ought to have a power on her head.' What is this, to have a power on her head? It is a manner of speaking in Scripture ... to have a sign and token of power, which is by covering her head."[27]

Both John Calvin, who founded the Continental Reformed Churches, and John Knox, the founder of the Presbyterian Church, advocated for women wearing headcoverings. John Calvin believed that headcoverings were fundamental to modesty for Christian women, and warned that those who removed their

---

[25] Susan Karant-Nunn and Merry E. Wiesner-Hanks. 2012. Luther on Women: A Sourcebook. Cambridge, UK: Cambridge University Press, 95.

[26] Martin Luther. A Sermon on Marriage, 15 January 1525 WA XVII/I – Quoted from Susan C. Karant-Nunn & Merry E. Wiesner – Luther on Women: A Sourcebook (Cambridge University Press, 2003) page 95. Treadwell, John H. Martin Luther (London: Marcus Ward & Co, 1881), 217.

[27] The Sermons of Hugh Latimer, Volume 1 (London: J. Scott, 1758), 280–281.

veils might eventually remove their clothing, leading to immodesty.[28] John Calvin also comments on 1 Corinthians 11:2–16 by saying, "Women ought to have their heads covered when they pray or prophesy; otherwise, they dishonor their head. For as the man honors his head by showing his liberty, so the woman, by showing her subjection. Hence, on the other hand, if the woman uncovers her head, she shakes off subjection."[29] In a sermon on 1 Corinthians, Calvin gets explicit on the matter by saying:

> So if women are thus permitted to have their heads uncovered and to show their hair, they will eventually be allowed to expose their entire breasts, and they will come to make their exhibitions as if it were a tavern show; they will become so brazen that modesty and shame will be no more; in short they will forget the duty of nature.... Further, we know that the world takes everything to its own advantage. So, if one has liberty in lesser things, why not do the same with this the same way as with that? And in making such comparisons they will make such a mess that there will be utter chaos. So, when it is permissible for the women to uncover their heads, one will say, 'Well, what harm in uncovering the stomach also?' And then after that one will plead for something else; 'Now if the women go bareheaded, why not also bare this

---

28 "Christian Head Covering." n.d. Wikipedia. Accessed March 18, 2023. https://en.wikipedia.org/wiki/Christian_head_covering.

29 John Calvin. n.d. "Commentary on 1 Corinthians 11:2–16 Regarding Headcoverings." Covenanter.org. Accessed February 23, 2023. https://www.covenanter.org/reformed/2015/7/15/john-calvins-commentary-on-1-corinthians-112-16.

and bare that?" Then the men, for their part, will break loose too. In short, there will be no decency left, unless people contain themselves and respect what is proper and fitting, so as not to go headlong overboard.[30]

In the 1500–1600s, the Puritans were an incredible example of Christian piety. Named for their extreme commitment to purifying out all that was unbiblical, the Puritans produced some of the church's greatest theologians. Men like John Bunyan (author of Pilgrim's Progress), John Owen, Thomas Watson, Jeremiah Burroughs, Matthew Henry, and many more. It is well known by their paintings, writings, and teachings that headcoverings were an undisputed doctrine of the Church. One of my favorite Puritans, John Cotton, said, "All the members of the Church... are to join together... the men with their heads uncovered, the women covered."[31]

In the 16th and 17th centuries, both the Church of England and The Augsburg Confession of Lutheran Churches affirm headcoverings. The Augsburg Confession states, "Paul ordains, 1 Cor. 11:5, that women should cover their heads in the congregation... It is proper that the churches should keep such ordinances for the sake of love and tranquility."[32]

---

30 Seth Skolnitsky, John Calvin. 1992. Sermon on 1 Cor 11:2–3. (Philidelphia, PA: Presbyterian Heritage Publications), Pg. 12–13.

31 John Cotton. (1642) 2008. The True Constitution of a Particular Visible Church. Shropshire, England: Quinta Press.

32 Philipp Melanchthon. 2011. The Augsburg Confession: Article 28:54–55. Tredition Classics.

Methodism's founder, John Wesley, also thought that a woman should wear a veil, especially in religious settings. He says, "Therefore if a woman is not covered—If she will throw off the badge of subjection, let her appear with her hair cut like a man's. But if it be shameful for a woman to appear thus in public, especially in a religious assembly, let her, for the same reason, keep on her veil."[33] Other Reformation-era Methodist theologians like Thomas Coke, Adam Clarke, Joseph Sutcliffe, Joseph Benson, and Walter Ashbel Sellew agreed with the traditional understanding of 1 Corinthians 11, which says that women should wear veils and men shouldn't wear hats when they pray.

Jonathan Edwards, the esteemed preacher of the first Great Awakening during the 1730s, wrote on the issue of headcoverings, "Paul's will is that the Corinthian men, who were converts and saints, should be bare-headed in their religious assemblies. And from St. Paul, all Christians generally have received and practiced this usage... The Christian Churches at this day conform to this usage... That which the Apostle delivers in this chapter concerning women's behavior in the churches did not only oblige the women of that time but is obligatory to this very day. All Christian women are engaged by virtue of what the Apostle here saith, to be always with their heads covered in a time of prayer and other religious exercises."[34]

---

33 John Wesley. 1990. Wesley's Notes on the Bible. Grand Rapids, MI: Zondervan.

34 John Edwards. (1692) 2011. An Enquiry into Four Remarkable Texts of the New Testament Which Contain Some Difficulty in Them, with a Probable Resolution of Them. Proquest, Eebo Editions.

This interpretation continues on through the works of many influential theologians and pastors, including the Cambridge scholar Joseph Mede, the English pastor Thomas Wall, and the Presbyterian preacher R.L. Dabney.[35] It also continued among several denominational groups and protestant associations, including the Moravian Church (an early form of the Methodist church), the Anglican Church, and the London Presbyterians (a group associated with the Westminster Assembly).[36]

The Baptist heritage is not without mention here, too. In fact, an influential advocate for headcovering was Roger Williams, the founder of the first Baptist church in North America. He aligned this practice with the customs of the early Church.[37] The Prince of Preachers—the great Charles Spurgeon, held to the observance of headcoverings for women. In a sermon on Angels, he preached, "The reason why our sisters appear in the House of God with their heads covered is 'because of the angels.' The apostle says that a woman is to have a covering upon her head because of the angels."[38]

Having said that, it would be dishonest not to disclose the few but prominent theologians of the Reformation era

---

[35] James Dodson. 2016. "The Public Preaching of Women. — Reformed Presbyterian Church (Covenanted) - 'Steelite' Covenanters." Reformed Presbyterian Church (Covenanted) - "Steelite" Covenanters. May 24, 2016.

[36] Renee Ellison. 2022. The Biblical Headcovering: Scarf of Hidden Power. Arizona: Independent Publishing.

[37] Carla Gardina Pestana. 2004. Quakers and Baptists in Colonial Massachusetts. Cambridge, England: Cambridge University Press.

[38] C.H. Spurgeon. 1996. Spurgeon's Sermons on Angels. Grand Rapids, MI: Kregel Publications.

who did not adhere to this doctrine. The most notable was John Calvin's successor Theodore Beza who said, "By this he [Paul] gathers that if men do either pray or preach in public assemblies having their heads covered (which was a sign of subjection), they robbed themselves of their dignity, against God's ordinance.... It appears, that this was a political law serving only for the circumstances of the time that Paul lived in, by this reason, because in our days for a man to speak bareheaded in an assembly is a sign of subjection."[39] Ultimately, Beza saw the command as a cultural custom that does not apply to other cultures or time periods. Bible commentator Matthew Poole and Anglican theologian William Whitaker hold this position, too. I will deal with this argument extensively in chapter five.

Westminster Divine Herbert Palmer and Geneva-Italian reformer Francis Turretin also claim it as a local custom relating it to the category of command to abstain from eating blood found in Acts 15:29 at the Jerusalem council.[40] I will address this line of reasoning in several places within my commentary as well.

However, by and large, headcoverings for women were still the normative practice in the church until the early 1900s. To find a congregation in this era where women appeared uncovered

---

[39] Theodore Beza. 1599. The New Testament of Our Lord Iesus Christ : Translated out of Greeke by Theod. Beza ; with Brief Summaries and Expositions upon the Hard Places by the Said Authour, Ioac. Camer., and P. Lofeler Villerius ; Englished by L. Tomson ; with Annotations of Fr. Iunius upon Revelation. London: Deputies of Christopher Barker.

[40] Herbert Palmer, Cawdrey, Daniel. Sabbatum Redivivum: Or, the Christian Sabbath Vindicated, in a Full Discourse Concerning the Sabbath and the Lords Day. United Kingdom: R. White, 1645.

would be extremely difficult, if not impossible. But, even with an enormous and unified position on this doctrine, there began a flicker of resistance as feminism began to gain momentum in the 19th century. I will discuss this in the following chapter.

Modern Proponents of Headcovering

As for the 20th and 21st centuries, there have been a handful of faithful men and women who have held the line on this vital biblical doctrine. The late Dr. R. C. Sproul (1939–2017) taught the practice of headcoverings in several sermons and teachings but defended the practice and his interpretation in his book *Knowing Scripture*. In his book *Essential Truths of the Christian Faith*, he records, "During my high school years when I went to church on Sunday morning, I never saw a woman in that church whose head wasn't covered with a hat or a veil. That is one of those customs that has simply disappeared for the most part from Christian culture."[41] In a sermon, he defends his reason for upholding the practice of headcoverings by saying, "If anything transcends local customs, it is those things that are rooted and ordered in creation. That's why I'm very frightened to be loose with this passage."[42]

There is an emerging group of pastors, seminarians, and theologians who, by God's grace, have been raised up to teach and revive this important doctrine. The leading modern scholar

---

41 R.C. Sproul. 2021. Essential Truths of Christian Faith. Wheaton, IL: Tyndale House.

42 R.C. Sproul. "To Cover or Not to Cover." Ligonier. Accessed February 2023a.

on the topic is the late Dr. Leslie McFall, who died in 2015. He was a British scholar who was formerly a lecturer in Hebrew and the Old Testament before becoming a full-time researcher at Tyndale House, Cambridge. His incredible 579-page book *Good Order in the Church* is the most exhaustive and compelling defense of headcoverings ever written. Dr. Bruce Waltke of Dallas Theological Seminary and Dr. Phillip Kayser of Whitfield Theological Seminary has brought helpful modern contributions. In his book *Glory and Coverings*, Dr. Kayser says, "It brought tears to my eyes when I finally realized that I had unwittingly been teaching contrary to Paul's mandates in 1 Corinthians 11:1–16. It struck me like a ton of bricks that I had been honoring what Paul calls a "dishonor" and had been quite comfortable with a practice which Paul calls shameful."[43]

Now, while scholars are vital for restoring this doctrine to the church, it's pastors who diffuse these truths to the church body. My friend Brian Sauvé who pastors Refuge Church in Ogden, Utah, and his wife Lexy are doing this through their podcast *Bright Hearth*, where they discuss the biblical call for headcoverings. Other pastors like Joel Webbon of Right Response Ministries, Jeremy Gardiner of The Headcovering Movement, Eric Conn, Bnonn Tenant, and myself are also continuing to speak out with a pastoral tone and a heart for biblical reformation.

From the Old Testament Church Era to the present day,

---

43 Phillip Kayser. 2018. Glory and Covering: A Study of 1 Corinthians 11:1–16. United States: Biblical Blueprints.

history offers compelling evidence for the longstanding practice of headcoverings in the church. In the next chapter, we will delve deeper into the role of feminism and its suppression of the practice of headcoverings over the past 140 years. By understanding this important historical context, you will better comprehend the surrounding cultural pressures and will be able to make a more informed decision about headcoverings for your own life.

Chapter 03
FEMINISM AND THE FALLING AWAY OF HEADCOVERINGS

An idea that appears to be a seed of hope may initially inspire and motivate, but if it is based on falsehood, it will eventually grow into a weed that chokes out the truth and disrupts order in a garden.

In the late 1800s, first-wave feminism was that seed. It appeared as a message of hope advocating for women's rights and opportunities. But over time, it has shown itself as a weed that subverts God's design for order among genders.

Today, it is evident that feminism is about liberation, but liberation from what? Primarily of a woman's identity as man's helper and secondarily from motherhood and the keeping of a home (Gen. 2:18; Tit. 2:5). As we will see later in this book, Scripture says that Man is the image and glory of God while Woman is the glory of man (1 Cor. 11:7–8). Namely, Man was made *for* God and *from* God, while Woman is made *for* man and *from* man. Now, I stand with G. K. Chesterton, who famously said, "If I set the sun beside the moon, And if I set the land beside the sea, And if I set the flower beside the fruit, And if I set the town beside the country, And if I set the man beside the woman, I suppose some fool would talk about one being better."[44] In other words, God's distinct design for men and women does not mean men and women are unequal in value, but it does mean they are unequal in nature and role. This is a detestable truth to the feminist mind. As a result, it should not shock us that today's women who are now bathed in feminism's liberation doctrine would reject the practice of wearing physical symbols that represent feminine submission and biblical gender identity.

This is exactly what began to happen in the late 1800s and has carried on until the present. As the liberation movement gained momentum, feminists encouraged the removal of veils, headcoverings, bonnets, and hats. It was, in a real sense, the seeds of rebellion that have led to today's feminism that encourages the removal of bras and long hair. Gena Conti, a modern feminist, describing the disappearing of headcoverings said, "I think part of [removing headcoverings] had to do with women not wanting to be told what to do, darn it—not being told whether you have to be respectable, have to do this, do that.... It's like the statement with burning bras: get rid of a hat, you're free!"[45]

The question I would ask Ms. Conti is, "Free from what?" Free from God's design for men and women? Initially, this form

---

[44] G.K. Chesterton. 1994. Collected Works of G. K. Chesterton: Collected Poetry : Part 1 (Collected Works of Gk Chesterton). San Francisco, CA: Ignatius Press.

[45] Tao Tao Holmes. 2016. "When Going out without a Hat Was Grounds for Scandal." Atlas Obscura. March 21, 2016. https://www.atlasobscura.com/articles/when-going-out-without-a-hat-was-grounds-for-scandal.

FEMINISM & THE FALLING AWAY OF HEADCOVERINGS   43

of freedom is a thrill, but, as time passes, we have begun to realize that without the divine boundaries and structure for men and women, the result is gender chaos and confusion.

In the early 20th century, women started to adopt bonnets and decorative hats as a fashionable replacements for their headcoverings. This was a very subtle form of Christian feministic rebellion. It wasn't a rejection of the headcovering altogether; it was merely a modification to a more culturally acceptable expression. That is, for many, the priority was less about displaying a woman's station and more about conforming to the trends of the time.

In a feminist article titled *When Going Out Without a Hat Was Grounds for Scandal*, the author writes, "For a growing number of Western women, beginning in the 1920s and continuing up until the 1960s, a hat or headcovering felt like a symbol of control and regulation—a symbol of the rules created by men governing the bodies of women."[46] Namely, the headcovering and its religious roots became the enemy of liberation.

In 1927, a group of Spanish feminists rebelling against the influences of the Catholic Church in Spain formed a group called "Las Sinsombrero," which means "those without hats."[47] As a group, they became popular for their public refusal to conform to the gender norms of that era. This was, of course, an effort to further dismantle the symbols of religious life and biblical

---

46 Tao Tao Holmes. When Going out without a Hat Was Grounds for Scandal."

47 Wikipedia contributors. n.d. "Las Sinsombrero." Wikipedia, The Free Encyclopedia. https://es.wikipedia.org/w/index.php?title=Las_Sinsombrero&oldid=149441201.

gender identity in the public square.

Elizabeth Farians, who identifies as a Catholic but is known for her feminist activism against religious groups, formed a NOW task force in 1968 and called for a "National Unveiling" to protest the tradition of requiring women to cover their heads in church. The "Easter Bonnet Rebellion" took place on Easter Sunday at a Milwaukee church after a priest criticized a woman for her uncovered head. Fifteen women with outrageously large hats approached the communion rail, removed their hats, and received communion in what she claims is the "first church demonstration for women's rights."[48]

This rebellion and unveiling of women continued from the 1960s through the 1980s. Despite the fact that a headcovering is supposed to cover the head, the hats during this period progressively became smaller until they eventually disappeared. Luma Simms, in an article from 2013 on Christianity Today titled "Uncovering the Head Covering Debate," wrote, "The practice of head covering continued even up to the early 20th century... By the 1960s in the West, the biblical practice had become merely a tradition, so when hats fell out of style, the practice was dropped in Christian churches."[49]

The eradication of gender distinctions resulted in increased feminine independence, causing a decline in the number of women

---

[48] Elizabeth Farians: "Catholic Feminist Pioneer." n.d. Feminist Studies in Religion. Accessed February 23, 2023. https://www.fsrinc.org/elizabeth-farians/.

[49] Luma Simms. 2013. "Uncovering the Head Covering Debate." CT Women. October 1, 2013. https://www.christianitytoday.com/ct/2013/october-web-only/uncovering-head-covering-debate.html.

starting families and a rise in female participation in the workforce. As a consequence, chivalry, defined as "an honorable and courteous way of behavior, particularly towards women," began to disappear. Women, who had previously found clear identity and purpose in marriage, motherhood, and homemaking, were now single, pursuing careers, and lacking a framework for biblical roles and femininity.

I want you to see that for nearly twenty centuries, the church influenced the culture on gender roles and modesty with this practice. It's fairly uncommon to see an ancient, medieval, or historical painting or statue where a woman is not wearing a headcovering. Today, the tables have turned. Now, the culture has influenced the church on gender roles and modesty. As a result, headcoverings, and the biblical meaning behind them, have been lost in the annals of history and stripped from feminine culture. Consequently, most modern Christian women have never even heard of this biblical practice. If they have, their story is similar to my wife, who thought it was a tradition only continued by the Amish, Mennonites, and the oppressed women of the Middle East.

The feminist movement throughout history has sought to challenge and redefine traditional gender roles, striving for egalitarianism and individuality as opposed to the biblical order. This has led to confusion and disorder in terms of gender identity and roles. However, it is important to remember that while history has its place, our ultimate authority lies in Scripture. To truly understand the issue at hand, we must look to Scripture and not merely adopt the conclusions of others or conform to the narrative of a fallen culture.

To do this, let's delve into 1 Corinthians 11:2–16 and employ sound principles of interpretation, systematic exposition, and faithful grammatical exegesis. By engaging with the biblical text directly, we can uncover the truth of this Christian practice and offer a clear understanding rooted in Scripture itself.

Section Two

A DEFENSE FROM CONTEXT, SCRIPTURE AND DOCTRINE

Chapter 04

BUILDING CONFIDENCE WITH CONTEXT

For this book, I have decided to use the New American Standard Bible (1995 edition). The theological community generally accepts the NASB95 as the most accurate English translation.

Because Greek and English are not perfect crossover languages, translations like the NASB95 compromise readability for accuracy. Namely, it may seem clunky to read, but it's precise. Translations such as the ESV, however, offer greater readability but are not the best translation for exegetical accuracy.

As for the original language, I have studied and diagramed this passage in the Greek. I am aware of textual variants and the interpretive range that can come with Greek words. As for my method of interpretation, I am using what is called the Grammatical-Historical Method, which is an approach that takes the text literally within its proper context. This means I will be looking at the author, the date, the location, the audience, and the purpose of the correspondence. It also means I am studying the grammar, syntax, mood, and genre in an attempt to accurately extract Paul's original meaning in this passage. If you would like to learn more about how to carry out this type of biblical interpretation on your own, I wrote a short book called "The Ground of Good Theology," which breaks down this process in detail.

Outline of our Passage

Paul's writings are highly intellectual and theological and can be difficult to understand at times. Even the Apostle Peter thought this when he said in 2 Peter 3:15–16, "Just as also our beloved brother Paul, according to the wisdom given him, wrote to you, as also in all his letters, speaking in them of these things, in which are some things hard to understand, which the untaught and unstable distort, as they do also the rest of the Scriptures, to their own destruction." This is why it is helpful for us to organize the Apostle's words into categories or sections so that we can more accurately interpret the meaning of his words. Through diagramming the biblical text, I have broken this passage into seven sections. They are as follows:

Section #1: 11:2: A Praise for Obedience
Section #2: 11:3–6: An Argument from Authority
Section #3: 11:7–9: An Argument from Creation
Section #4: 11:10 An Argument from the Spiritual Realm
Section #5: 11:11–12: Men and Women Equal Before God
Section #6: 11:13–15: An Argument from Nature
Section #7: 11:16: An Argument from the Church
(You can see my full block diagram in Appendix B)

Historical and Cultural Context

The word "context" is made up of the two Latin words con and textus and literally means together-woven. So, the context is simply the setting in which a particular book or text has been woven. When you understand the context, you will better understand the content.

First Corinthians is a letter written by the Apostle Paul. The city of Corinth was a seaside town located in Southern Greece on an isthmus West of Athens by 45 miles.

Due to its location, trade and traffic were high, making Corinth a metropolitan town of its day filled with various cultural influences and people groups. Corinth's transient community and worldly influences had built a reputation of immorality and the cultivation of corruption. To give you a contemporary comparison, Corinth might be similar to modern-day San Francisco. The most prominent monument in the city was a temple dedicated to Aphrodite—the goddess of love. Over 1,000 prostitutes lived in the temple and would flood the streets each evening to serve the travelers entering the city.

Paul planted the Corinthian church during his second missionary journey (Acts 18:1) by preaching the Gospel in the local synagogues. Paul lived in Corinth for 18 months (Acts 18:11) until he was persecuted by Jewish leaders (which dissolved) and left for Ephesus. If you've read First Corinthians, you know the overwhelming immaturity, division, and sinfulness present among this community of believers. The letter is known as a letter of Christian ethics because the Apostle spends so much of his attention correcting inappropriate behavior. Ultimately, First Corinthians is a book of rich Christian instruction around a variety of practical issues. But most of all, it's a letter of love that is written with the heart and tone of a father.

Our particular passage (11:2–16) is in a section of the letter that marks a transition from discussing the balance between liberty and discretion as Christians and his instruction for corporate worship. In other words, our section is the letter's last teaching on common Christian life before Paul spends three chapters on corporate Christian life beginning in 11:17–14:40. You can see the transition to corporate life in 11:18 where he says, "For, in the first place, *when you come together as a church*, I hear that divisions exist among you; and in part, I believe it." At this point, the Apostle teaches on a variety of topics, including the Lord's Supper (11:17–34), spiritual gifts (12–13:25), and orderly church gatherings (14:26–40). This is important as we need to see this teaching on headcoverings as not only an application for our time during the Sunday assembly but also during the spiritual actions of everyday Christian life.

The Journey Ahead

For the next seven chapters, I will walk you through the seven sections of 1 Corinthians 11:2–16. In each section, we will examine the claims of those particular verses, and I will offer my commentary, defense, and application. By the time you're finished, you will have a robust grasp on the doctrine of headship, the creation account, and male and female roles in the family and church. At the close of the book, I will offer a conclusion and a small chapter on common questions for practical applications.

Chapter 05

A PRAISE FOR OBEDIENCE

1 Corinthians 11:2

"Now I praise you because you remember me in everything and hold firmly to the traditions, just as I delivered them to you."

The Apostle knows that a wise pastor does not only bring corrections without also bringing praise. After a long section of exhortation and instruction, the start of this paragraph must have been an encouragement to the Corinthians.

Apparently, the Corinthians had maintained an honorable degree of respect for Paul's words, teachings, customs, and traditions. We assume this was made clear in the letter the Corinthians wrote to Paul (which we do not have), by which 1 Corinthians is a response. It's very likely Paul was including the tradition of headcovering, and uncovering for men, in his praise. Namely, he is likely responding to particular questions or objections regarding this instruction of headwear. Practice without theological backing can lead to religiosity, and Paul never wants Christian action to be disconnected from biblical doctrine.

The word "traditions" in verse 2 has been used by some interpreters as an argument to reject the authority of this entire passage. They say, "This is not a matter of doctrine but a matter of local and ancient traditions." First, in the New Testament, *tradition* has a far more robust definition than our modern-day understanding. For example, in 2 Thessalonians 3:6, we see the same Greek word used by the same author with apostolic force and authority. He writes, "Now we command you, brethren, in the name of our Lord Jesus Christ, that you keep away from every brother who leads an unruly life and not according to the *tradition* which you received from us."

A few verses earlier in 2 Thessalonians 2:15, he also writes, "So then, brethren, stand firm and hold to the *traditions* which you were taught, whether by word of mouth or by epistle." In other words, apostolic traditions, especially those which are taught or commanded in Scripture, are not merely suggested practices of man but biblical and authoritative instructions from God's chosen messengers. I cannot stress this enough, the traditions established by God's Apostles are everlasting, particularly when they represent immutable realities such as the creation order or the angelic realm. In essence, these kinds of traditions are not grounded in man-made cultures but rather in a Kingdom culture being constructed by God Himself.

Corinthian or Kingdom Custom?

It is important to note that Paul is not talking about Corinthian traditions but the traditions that *he delivered to them*. Some commentators try to argue that headcovering for women and uncovering for men was merely the cultural custom of the day and, as a result, is null and void for modern Christians. Not only does Corinthian history prove otherwise, but Paul clarifies that this tradition of headcovering comes *not* from Corinth but from him, as an Apostle of Jesus Christ. In other words, the doctrine of headcoverings is not cultural but *counter-cultural* to the Corinthian customs of the day.

Corinth was a province of Rome. When we look at first-century Roman history and religious practice, we do not see men uncovering and women covering their heads during worship. In fact, we see the *exact* opposite. For example, on the "Via Labicana Augustus," a sculpture of the Roman Emperor Augustus who lived from 63 B.C.–14 A.D., you will find the inscription "Pontifex Maximus." In Latin, this means "High Priest." This statue, sculpted in 12 B.C., shows Augustus wearing a full-length headcovering. Namely, covering the head was the normative practice for the High Priest of Rome.[50]

In another sculpture titled "Relief of Monument in Honour of Divine Marcus Aurelius," you can see the Emperor sacrificing before the Temple of Jupiter while wearing a full-length headcovering. "Roman Antiquities," a historical text penned by Dionysius of Halicarnassus, a Greek historian from the early Roman Empire in the 1st century B.C., documents, "It was in

---

50 Finny Kuruvilla. 2018. The Headcovering #1: Cultural or Counter-Cultural. United States: YouTube. https://www.youtube.com/watch?v=QA4bxP0nY_0. (3-Part Series).

accordance with the traditional usages, then, that Camillus, after making his prayer and drawing his garment down over his head, wished to turn his back."[51] Plutarch records, "Why is it that when they worship the gods, they cover their heads, but when they meet any of their fellow-men worthy of honor, if they happen to have the toga over the head, they uncover?"[52] Ultimately, these become further evidence that the custom of the time was for men to cover their heads during acts of worship.

As for ancient Greek and Roman women, some biblical interpreters claimed Paul's teaching in 1 Corinthians 11:2–16 was a reaction to the number of disreputable women (prostitutes) who wandered about Corinth with uncovered heads. They imply that all respectable Greek women, like the Jews, wore headcoverings. Yet, this does not appear to be supported by any ancient sources.[53] (See footnote 53 for a full explanation). In Plutarch's

---

51 Dionysius Halicarnassensis. 1758 (English Edition). The Roman Antiquities. United Kingdom: University of Lausanne.

52 Plutarch. 2013. Romane Questions. United States: Rarebooksclub.com.

53 Bible research scholar Michael Marlow who studied at Pittsburgh Theological Seminary cites in his work "Headcovering Customs of the Ancient World": Many of the statements regarding Greek customs found in otherwise respectable commentaries reveal a surprising level of carelessness in the use of cultural background information. Unsupported speculations are often asserted as fact, and then repeated by other scholars. For example, G.G. Findlay, writing in The Expositor's Greek Testament (1900) states that "Amongst Greeks only the hetaerae [high-class prostitutes], so numerous in Corinth, went about unveiled" (vol. II, p. 872), but he gives no historical source for this assertion. This statement is quoted by A.T. Robertson in his Word Pictures in the New Testament (1933) without any indication of its being questionable (vol. IV, pp. 159-160), and from there it is quoted in several more recent books. But there is no historical basis for the assertion, and it is contradicted by some evidence. For ancient depictions of Greek women in public and in pagan worship services without headcoverings see Verena Zinserling, Women in Greece and Rome (New York:

Sayings of Spartans, written during the first century A.D., he writes, "When someone inquired why they took their girls into public places unveiled, but their married women veiled, he said, 'Because the girls have to find husbands, and the married women have to keep to those who have them!'"[54] Namely, there is no historical evidence to believe that Greco-Roman women were compelled to cover their heads in public or in worship lest they be identified as harlots. This idea is without a historical basis. Now, this does not mean that Greco-Roman women did not ever cover their heads—they did, but there is no clear cultural custom or religious purpose to do so.[55]

Bible researcher and historian Michael Marlowe cites in his article *Headcoverings in the Ancient World*:

> "Regarding [Greek] religious practices, there are clear indications that in some pagan religious observances it was the custom for women to take part with their heads uncovered. The cult of the goddess Demeter involved certain rites called the Eleusinian mysteries. A depiction of the Eleusinian mysteries on the Ninnion Tablet in the National Archaeological Museum of Athens shows women wearing only tiaras or leaf chaplets in their hair. In the Rule of the

---

Abner Schram, 1972).

54 Plutarch. 2018. Sayings of the Spartans. Translated by Frank Cole Babbit. Vol. 3. Vigeo Press.

55 Michael Marlow. 2005. "Headcoverings in the Ancient World." Bible Researcher. 2005. http://www.bible-researcher.com/headcoverings3.html.

Andanian Mysteries it is stipulated that the initiates "are all to be wreathed with laurel" and that none of the women are to wear a "hair band, or braided hair." In the worship of Dionysus, the female celebrants known as *maenads* not only came with uncovered heads but also let down their hair and danced in the public processions. Many ancient paintings show women presenting offerings at altars—probably as priestesses—without headcoverings."[56]

Furthermore, the cultic order of Lycosura seems to forbid the veiling of women as empresses, and goddesses are always portrayed without veils.[57] During the reign of Augustus, the cult of Isis, originating from Egypt, gained popularity, particularly among women. Within its ceremonies, the priests would cover their heads, while priestesses would not. A picture of a sculpture of an Isaic procession can be found in Arnold Toynbee's *Crucible of Christianity*.[58]

Secular author Richard Oster in an essay titled "When Men Wore Veils to Worship: The Historical Context of 1 Corinthians 11:4," published by Cambridge Press, surveys the cities of the ancient Roman Empire and offers overwhelming evidence that the cultural practice of the day was for men to cover their heads

---

[56] Michael Marlow. 2005. "Headcoverings in the Ancient World."

[57] Kittel, G., and Gerhard Friedrich, eds. 1959. Theological Dictionary of the New Testament. Translated by Geoffrey W. Bromiley. Grand Rapids, MI: William B Eerdmans Publishing, Vol. 3 Pg. 562.

[58] Arnold Toynbee. 1969. Crucible of Christianity. London, England: Thames & Hudson. Pg. 238.

and women to uncover their heads during Roman worship.[59]

In sum, Paul's teaching here in 1 Corinthians 11:2–16 is not simply affirming the religious customs of Corinth; it was instructing a *new* Christian practice that was the *exact opposite* of the religious customs of Corinth. As we have seen, the Greco-Roman practice was that men cover their heads during worship and women uncover, making it antithetical to the instructions written here in 1 Corinthians 11:2–16.

It's very possible that the Corinthian men and women were tempted to mirror the worship of the pagan customs of the day by inappropriately covering and uncovering their heads during spiritual activities. I believe Paul's motive was to establish a new Christian order, anchored in creation and unchanging gender distinctions as a way to reorient the church from the disorder of the cults.

The "Corinthian cultural argument," which claims that this practice is specific to Corinthian culture, is further weakened when we consider that Paul's guidelines for uncovering and covering were not in line with either Greco-Roman or Jewish religious practices. The command of the Old Testament priest was also to cover his head (Exodus 29:6). Rabbis and common Jewish men wore a Tallit (a prayer shawl). To this day, Jewish men wear a yamaka during spiritual functions.

---

[59] Oster, Richard. 1988. When Men Wore Veils to Worship: The Historical Context of 1 Corinthians 11.4. New Testament Studies 34, No. 4. Cambridge, UK: Cambridge University Press. If you want even more evidence against the cultural argument you can read Dr. Ben Witherington's work titled "Conflict and Community in Corinth: A Socio-Rhetorical Commentary on 1 and 2 Corinthians."

The immediate question becomes: Why did priests in the Old Testament cover their heads, and men in the New Testament are prohibited from covering their heads? In the Old Covenant, God the Father was the head of man, and man (specifically the high priest), could not approach His presence with his head uncovered (Exod. 39:27 Jerusalem Bible; cf. also Exod. 28:40; 29:9; Lev. 8:9, 13). Christ was born as a man, with God the Father as His head (1 Cor. 11:3), to establish the new and superior Covenant (Heb. 8:6). He took on the role of High Priest and mediator between God and humanity, offering a single sacrifice for sins and granting humanity access to the Most Holy Place (Heb. 10:12, 19–20). In short, Christ's New Covenant ministry replaced the Old Covenant priesthood that required covered heads. Dr. McFall asserts:

> We now have access to the Holy of Holies through a High Priest who is the perfect "image and glory of God," and who, therefore, ought not to have His head covered. He is also perfect man and worships God with an uncovered head, therefore his brothers are encouraged not to cover their heads when they worship in the presence of God (1 Cor. 11:4, 7; cf. Heb. 2:11).[60]

The evidence does not fit the claim that headcoverings were merely an affirmation or clarification of the cultural practice

---

60 Leslie McFall. 2002. Good Order in the Church: The Head of Man Is Christ, The Head of Woman Is Man. England: Self-Published, Pg. 27.

of the day. The evidence points us to conclude that Paul was introducing a new Christian practice that stood in opposition to the existing religious practice of their day. This explains the challenges Corinthians faced in adopting the practice and their need to seek Paul's clarification on the matter.

In the next chapter, you will see Paul anchor the reasons for this entire teaching on headcovering not in local or early church customs, but in the unchanging, eternal truths of the creation order of man and woman, divine authority, and angelic witness. In other words, Paul is going to give us the theological grounds for the practice of headcoverings. This is an important distinction because when the reasons for the practice are unchanging, the practice must also be unchanging.

Chapter 06

AN ARGUMENT FROM AUTHORITY

1 Corinthians 11:3-6

Before I was in ministry, I led two successful companies, wrote two bestselling business books, and was involved in corporate strategy. In my book *People Over Profit*, I researched organizational structures.

At the time, there was a new movement toward "Co-Ceo's" emerging among startups. I critiqued the practice harshly as all historical institutions proved that such dual-led structures would never permit a company to thrive. There is no country with two kings, no military company with two Captains, and no universities with two presidents, and for good reason.

The same logic is true with the structure for the family. Two husbands cannot work, not just because they are sexually incompatible but also because men have unique roles to lead within a marriage. The same can be said of two wives because women have unique roles to submit, help, and follow. In a marriage with two men or two women, these roles cannot be accomplished without one party playing the role of the opposite sex. In other words, dual leadership does not work. I say all of that to show that when we attempt to equalize roles and remove God-given distinctions regarding order, we end up causing unworkable institutions that do not thrive.

These examples serve as a fundamental basis for our discussion, as we will observe in this part of our text that God is a God of order (1 Cor. 14:33). Elisabeth Elliot, in her book *The Essense of Femininity*, brings our attention to the wisdom and beauty of God's order when she wrote, "I see the arrangement of the universe and the full harmony and tone of Scripture. This arrangement is a glorious hierarchical order of graduated splendor, beginning with the Trinity descending through seraphim, cherubim, archangels, angels, men, and all lesser creatures, a mighty universal dance, choreographed for the perfection and fulfillment of each participant."[61]

The order that God has assigned, regardless of our station, is beautiful, perfect, and wise. This is the posture we must have while trying to understand this passage of Scripture.

NEXT PORTION OF THE TEXT

1 Corinthians 11:3

But I want you to understand that Christ is the head of

---

[61] Elliot, Elisabeth. 2021. Recovering Biblical Manhood and Womanhood: A Response to Evangelical Feminism (Chapter: The Essence of Femininity: A Personal Perspective). Edited by John Piper and Wayne Grudem. Wheaton, IL: Crossway Books. 394.

every man, and the man is the head of a woman, and God is the head of Christ.

The Perfect Order of Creation

In 1 Corinthians 11:3–6, Paul introduces the discussion of headcoverings by anchoring his reasoning to the channels of authority set forth in creation. Namely, God has laid out an engendered authority structure that can be seen both in the creation account of Genesis (Gen. 1–3) and in the doctrine of headship and submission throughout the New Testament (e.g., Eph. 5:22–30; 1 Pet. 3:7; Col. 3:8, 1 Tim. 3:1–7; Gen. 3:16; 1 Tim. 2:11–15; Titus 1:5–9; 1 Cor. 14:34, etc.).

In this text, Paul uses the analogy of the body to illustrate his case. The body is subordinate to the work of the head and makes this concept plain for us to comprehend. As it pertains to *authority*, Christ is subordinate to the Father, men (males) are subordinate to Christ (who is their authority), and women (females) are subordinate to men (husbands, fathers, elders, etc., who is their authority). God places women under the rule and direction of men. These are channels of derived authority that demonstrate the structure of the Kingdom of God here on earth. When a man submits to the authority of Christ, he is submitting to God. When a woman submits to the authority of the men in her life (husband, father, or elder), she is, indeed, submitting to Christ and, ultimately, to God. This topic is robust and will not be the focus of this chapter, but I will make a few important points.

To begin, I understand that the term "headship" may evoke negative reactions, particularly for women who have been hurt by men. However, fourth-century theologian John Chrysostom highlights a crucial distinction regarding Paul's metaphor of the head and the body. Instead of using a master-slave analogy, Paul emphasizes the interconnectedness of the head and the body. They do not compete or conflict with one another; they function as a single unit, requiring collaboration and mutual care. This relationship significantly differs from that of separate entities like a master and slave. It embodies an inseparable union and love, rather than power and oppression.

Next, the subordination of Christ to the Father is far different from the subordination of women to men. As we know, human submission is carried out by sinners, while divine submission is not. Therefore, the submission of a woman to a man has limitations. For instance, a woman does not have to submit to a man forcing her to sin against God. The same limitation applies regarding the Christian's submission to the civil government. That is, the Bible clearly calls Christians to submit to the civil magistrate (Rom. 13; 1 Pet. 2:13–25), but we must not submit when that magistrate tells us to deny Christ, violate the Scriptures, or wound our conscience (Acts 5:29).

Submission is to recognize a legitimate authority over ourselves. In our culture of "girl bosses" and career women who are hungry for power, the biblical order can make a woman feel cheated. This is where Scripture must rule over our emotions. Let me show you why.

In the earthly ministry of Christ, we see Him willingly and even joyfully submitting to the Father. In John 6:38, Jesus says, "For I have come down from heaven, not to do my own will but the will of Him who sent me." Namely, Christ is an equal to the Father, yet, on earth, He willingly submits Himself out of love. This teaches us that submission can occur among equals. In fact, if you look at the text in 11:3, it says, "But I want you to understand that Christ is the head of every man, and the man is the head of a woman, and God is the head of Christ." Doesn't this seem like an odd way of stating structure? Wouldn't you say, "God is the head of Christ, Christ is the head of man, and man is the head of woman?" I believe Paul uses this structure to make a word picture for women to see this point. If we made the text into a diagram, it would look something like this:[62]

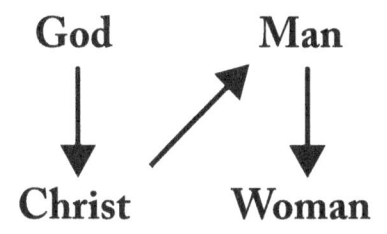

```
God        Man
 |        ↗ |
 ↓       /  ↓
Christ    Woman
```

Paul is offering a literary illustration that displays submission among equals and the mutual love that makes that submission possible. In a very real sense, Paul is implying to men and women, The relationship between the Father and the Son is built on

---

62 This diagram is from Finny Kuruvilla in Part #1 of a YouTube video titled "The Headcovering: Cultural or Counter-Cultural"

love, and because you have that same love, men and women can model a similar order. This loving arrangement between men and women is to be an extension and an image of the loving order we see among the members of the Trinity. In our world where relationships between men and women are disordered and broken, the example of God's loving authority and Christ's joyful submission becomes the model for our efforts.

It is important to notice that God has not put this structure of authority in place without reason. God uses structure to accomplish His will. For example, the work of the Gospel could not have occurred had God been tyrannical or had Christ been insubordinate. It was, in part, their commitment to a structure of authority that accomplished the work of redemption. The same is true of the authority structure for men and women. When we carry out our appointed identities, authorities, and roles in love, our lives will be fruitful and productive for the Kingdom of God. If we fail to conform to these identities, authorities, and roles, we get chaos and fruitlessness. This is clearly seen in the confusion and disarrangement of the LGBTQ[1] community. That is, homosexual structures are built upon perverse and inoperative realities that prohibit biblical order and biological reproduction. Therefore, it is vital that we see God's order as a benefit to us and not a limitation.

We must all remember that men did not choose to be the head of women, but, as a sex, men were endowed with this station by the Creator. For this reason, there is no room for men to boast about this privilege of authority. This simple fact should,

AN ARGUMENT FROM AUTHORITY   71

by God's grace, cause men to feel the weight of responsibility that comes from having such authority. Furthermore, women can feel reassured and valued in their position within this chain of authority, as it was established by a holy and all-wise God who ensures their well-being and significance.[63]

Both women and men have been designed biologically, spiritually, and emotionally to carry out the glorious stations given to them. For example, men are intrinsically wired to rule. In sin, they have become passive, but, at their core, they have been fraught with the dominating power of testosterone and a larger frame to protect and even physically carry the other sex. Women, on the other hand, lay down their lives in childbearing and nursing, they lay down their names in marriage, and they even lay down their bodies to receive the seed of man in intercourse.

Elisabeth Elliot once said of this, "Femininity receives. It says, 'May it be to me as you have said.' It takes what God gives—a special place, a special honor, a special function, and glory, different from that of masculinity, meant to be a help. In other words, it is for us women to receive 'the given' as Mary did, not to insist on the not-given, as Eve did."[64]

Women are receivers and surrenderers. They are intrinsically designed to follow and do it well. God has not cruelly

---

[63] Dr. McFall. Good Order in the Church. (Paraphrased from the Introduction, pages 4–5).

[64] Elisabeth Elliot. https://www.ligonier.org/learn/articles/let-me-be-woman Originally from "Recovering Biblical Manhood & Womanhood ed. by John Piper and Wayne Grudem, copyright © 1991, 397–399. Used by permission of Good News Publishers/Crossway Books, Wheaton, IL."

commanded from women tasks which they are not designed to do. The Lord has graciously given women (and men) all that they need to carry out their station to the glory of God. Ultimately, embracing God's design resembles a person who has been singing off-key. As they accept their biblical role and align with their intended purpose, they find the right pitch, achieving harmony with God's plan and experiencing deep joy and fulfillment.

In the following verse, you will see how the practice of headcoverings serves as a means for Christian men and women to visibly symbolize the authority structures we just discussed.

NEXT PORTION OF THE TEXT

1 Corinthians 11:4-5
Every man who has something on his head while praying or prophesying disgraces his head. But every woman who has her head uncovered while praying or prophesying disgraces her head, for she is one and the same as the woman whose head is shaved.

After laying the theological groundwork for spiritual authority, Paul introduces physical practices and symbols that represent these scriptural truths. It's important to note that the Apostle uses the term "head" interchangeably, meaning both the head in authority and the head of a physical body. He says, "Every man who has something on his physical head while praying or prophesying disgraces his spiritual head (that is, Christ—his spiritual authority)." He also says a woman who has her physical head uncovered while praying or prophesying disgraces her head (that is, Man, e.g., her husband, father, or elder—her spiritual authority).

Prayer and Prophecy Defined

Most of us know what it means to pray, but for the sake of precision, I'll offer you a definition from the Westminster Larger Catechism. It defines prayer this way, "Prayer is an offering up of our desires unto God, in the name of Christ, by the help of his Spirit; with confession of our sins, and thankful acknowledgment of his mercies."[65]

Prayer can be private or corporate. For example, when the saints gather on Sunday, and the pastor offers a prayer during the meeting, the members of the congregation are not simply passively listening but are co-praying in agreement with his words. This is why we say "amen" (which means "I agree") at the conclusion of his prayer. That is to say, this instruction regarding headcoverings is to be applied to both private and corporate prayer.

As for prophesying, there are two general definitions of the term. In the Old Testament, the term meant "to foretell the future or command God's people by the inspirations of the Holy Spirit according to God's perfect will." This is best seen in the ministries of men like Isaiah, Jeremiah, Ezekiel, David, Daniel,

---

[65] The Westminster Larger Catechism: Extended Annotated Edition. Question 178: What Is Prayer? 2012. Altenmünster, Germany: Jazzybee Verlag.

etc. To give you a sense of the gravity that came with claiming to be one of God's prophets, the Old Testament teaches that any "prophet" whose prophecies did not manifest perfectly should be stoned to death as a false prophet (Deut. 18:21–23).

However, Hebrews 1:1–2 tells us that this old form of prophecy has ended with the ministry of Christ and His Apostles. It says, "Long ago, at many times and in many ways, God spoke to our fathers by the prophets, but in these last days, he has spoken to us by his Son." That is, Christ is the last Prophet, and His Gospel is the last prophecy that we should expect from God.

Therefore, in the New Testament age, with the outpouring of the Holy Spirit upon believers and the completion of the Scriptures, the act of prophesying is a forth-telling of the Gospel according to the Word of God. Essentially, New Testament prophesying is recommunicating the last prophecy—the Gospel of Jesus Christ. We must remember that in Corinth, these believers did not have a copy of the New Testament Scriptures as we do today. They couldn't simply read the Gospel to one another. Instead, they relied on verbally retelling the Gospel by memory with the guidance of the Holy Spirit. This act fostered a deep, personal connection to the message of Christ, as they actively engaged in passing on the sacred teachings from one person to another.

Today, with the completion of the Scriptures, prophecy becomes a Holy Spirit-prompted proclamation that agrees with Scripture. This act can occur in various forms. For example, pulpit preaching at the gathering of the local church is certainly a form of prophesying and is the one form of prophecy that is forbidden for women (which we will discuss momentarily). In fact, one of my favorite books on preaching is *The Art of Prophesying* by the great Puritan theologian William Perkins. But prophesying could also be evangelism, reading Scripture aloud to children, and even singing aloud songs of Gospel truth. In fact, even partaking in the Lord's Supper is a form of prophesying because, as Paul says in 1 Corinthians 11:26, "For as often as you eat this bread and drink the cup, you *proclaim* the Lord's death until he comes."

Dr. Finny Kuruvilla, in his defense of headcoverings, makes an important point regarding this act of praying and prophesying. He points out that sacred and significant moments always call for a gender-specific dress. For example, a wedding calls for unique apparel for the bride and groom. For the bride, there are veils and garters and, of course, a beautiful white dress. For the groom, there is a suit, bowtie, and vest. The same is true for special occasions like the Opera, symphony, awards ceremonies, or a ball. Sacred and special events historically accentuate gender distinctions in clothing. If this alteration of engendered attire occurs in our common life, then how much more might this practice play out in our spiritual life? In other words, the concept of modifying our headwear during sacred and significant moments is not all that unusual.

As I mentioned above, Scripture forbids women to preach and teach in the Sunday assembly of the church (1 Tim. 2:12; 1 Cor. 14:34). In fact, Scripture lays the responsibility of preaching and theological instruction firmly at the feet of men (1 Tim.

3:1–16; Titus 1:6–9; Eph. 6:4). Since our text is in 1 Corinthians, let's consider Paul's prohibition of women preaching just a few chapters after our passage.

1 Corinthians 14:34–35

The women are to keep silent in the churches; for they are not permitted to speak, but are to subject themselves, just as the Law also says. If they desire to learn anything, let them ask their own husbands at home; for it is improper for a woman to speak in church.

I would like to first deal with a common misunderstanding of liberal readers of 1 Corinthians. These commentators use our passage in chapter eleven on headcoverings to discredit Paul's instruction of women remaining silent in the church in chapter fourteen. They say something like, "1 Corinthians 14:34–35 cannot be a complete prohibition of women teaching in the local church because, in chapter eleven, Paul explicitly states that women can pray and prophesy as long as they do so with their head covered."

Again, as I mentioned in chapter four, 1 Corinthians 14:34–35 sits within a section of the epistle that is dealing with the matters of *corporate* worship. Our passage in 1 Corinthians 11:2–16 sits in the last section of instructions for *common* Christian life. That is to say, context really does matter. The Bible *does not* prohibit women from praying and prophesying. But the Bible certainly prohibits women from leading prayer and preaching during the Sunday assembly, and thereby taking spiritual authority over a man (1 Cor. 14:34–35; 1 Tim. 2:8–12). In addition, Ephesians 5:22–33 clearly teaches the submission of wives and the duty of spiritual shepherding of husbands. This is indisputable. Therefore, if a woman is not permitted to spiritually shepherd her own husband, she is certainly not permitted to spiritually shepherd other women's husbands. No, God has established a design for spiritual authority, which is implemented consistently in both the family and the local church.

All that to say, Paul is not a schizophrenic who says one thing in chapter eleven and the opposite in chapter fourteen. He understands that women can pray and prophesy in common Christian life, and when they do so, they should cover their physical heads to symbolize their station in God's spiritual authority structure. Paul also knows that women can co-pray and partake in corporate forms of prophecy through singing and communion during the local assembly in a manner that does not grasp at the spiritual authority given to men.

Scripture does not contradict itself. Paul is simply offering clarity of application on a multi-dimensional issue. Interpreting Scripture accurately often requires a careful mind and a theologically trained teacher. There is a reason God gave to the Church, "the apostles, the prophets, the evangelists, the shepherds and teachers, to equip the saints for the work of ministry" (Eph. 4:11–12).

To return to headcoverings, Paul instructs both men and women how to properly display God's spiritual authority structure through the uncovering and covering of the physical head during prayer and prophecy.

CURRENT PORTION OF THE TEXT

1 Corinthians 11:4-5

Every man who has something on his head while praying or prophesying disgraces his head. But every woman who has her head uncovered while praying or prophesying disgraces her head, for she is one and the same as the woman whose head is shaved.

Uncovering for the Men

Paul says, "Every man who has something on his head while praying or prophesying disgraces his head." When a man prays or prophesies with his head covered, he is showing disrespect towards Christ, who is his head. This is because the man has been endowed with a specific authority and is the image and glory of God (1 Cor. 11:7). By covering his head, he indicates submission rather than dominion and conceals his glory instead of allowing it to be displayed. John Gill adds:

> "It was a custom in some nations for the men to worship their deities with their heads covered; and there were some philosophers among the Greeks that did so ... because it was a sign of subjection to their idols, and that they were under them, and in their power, and at their disposal; and

therefore was not to be done by the man, who is the image and glory of God, and who is to be uncovered in worship, to show that he is under the power and authority of no other than God, who is his head, and to whom only he is to be subject…he ought to appear as the image and glory of God, and as representing him, and as one having power and authority in his name; and therefore, when he [prays or prophesies] with his head covered, he dishonors his head, or Christ, whose name, and place, and authority he bears."[66]

Ultimately, for a man to cover his head during worship is to misrepresent his station, authority, and glory in God's order. To do so compromises the dignity of Christ, who is his head.

Practically speaking, I have never found a Christian man fighting against this teaching. Go to any rodeo across the United States and see how many men take off their hats during the opening prayer. Go to any Nascar race and watch the wave of men remove their caps as the announcer commences his petition to God for safety. Have you ever seen a pastor preach on Sunday with a hat on? Have you seen a farmer pray for his lunch with his head covered? Even pagan men follow this biblical teaching.

One might think that if Christian men unanimously agreed that the instruction for uncovering their heads while praying and prophesying is still a valid and binding biblical command, then

---

[66] John Gill. 1746. "Gill's Exposition of the Entire Bible. Commentary on 1 Corinthians 11 . 1999." Study Light. 1746. https://www.studylight.org/commentaries/eng/geb/1-corinthians-11.html.

the instruction for women to cover their heads while praying or prophesying would also be viewed as a valid and binding biblical command. Shockingly, it is not.

Dr. Michael Barrett, who is the Academic Dean at Puritan Reformed Theological Seminary, said of this inconsistency, "Although the requirements for man and woman are stated with equal clarity and authority, they have not received equal obedience. Whereas there are few men who would be so irreverent as to wear a hat during worship, there are many women who demonstrate equal irreverence by worshipping with uncovered heads."[67] I believe the reason for this inconsistency will become more clear as we continue through this book.

NEXT PORTION OF THE TEXT

1 Corinthians 11:5
But every woman who has her head uncovered while praying or prophesying disgraces her head, for she is one and the same as the woman whose head is shaved.

Covering for the Women
The text is saying that an uncovered woman during the acts of prayer and prophecy is to be viewed as a woman who has her hair shaved off. Two points need to be made here to understand

---

[67] Michael Barrett P. V. 2003. Headcovering for Public Worship: An Exposition of 1 Corinthians 11:2–16. Greenville, CS: Faith Free Presbyterian Church. https://www.headcoveringmovement.com/Michael-Barrett-Head-Covering-for-Public-Worship.pdf.

what is being said.

First, a woman with a shaved head in the first century was either because she was a prostitute, an adulteress, or unclean. In other words, it wasn't a good look for a woman.

Second, a woman without hair is visually unnatural and undesirable to men. Not only is this an intrinsically known fact, but it has been statistically proven. Tamás Bereczkei, Ph.D., professor of psychology, performed a study in which images of female faces were given varying lengths of hair and then evaluated by men on their attractiveness. She said, "Longer hair had a significant positive effect on the ratings of a woman's attractiveness; shorter styles did not."[68]

It is historically and statistically acknowledged that it is unwomanly for a female to have her head shaved. Therefore, Paul is saying that a woman who refuses to cover her head while praying or prophesying is as appalling of a sight as a woman whose head is shaved. John Calvin says of this verse, "In disapproving of the one (the shaved woman), he does not approve of the other (the uncovered woman)."[69] In a sense, Paul is saying that women who refuse to cover their heads put themselves in the same class as those women who shave their heads. Princeton theologian Charles Hodge said, "She assumes the characteristic

---

[68] Tamás Bereczkei, Norbert Meskó. 2006. "Hair Length, Facial Attractiveness, Personality Attribution: A Multiple Fitness Model of Hairdressing." https://www.researchgate.net/publication/235933312_Hair_length_facial_attractiveness_personality_attribution_A_multiple_fitness_model_of_hairdressing.

[69] John Calvin. 2022. Commentary, Vol. 1: On the Epistles of Paul the Apostle to the Corinthians (Classic Reprint). London, England: Forgotten Books.

mark of a disreputable woman."[70]

You cannot escape the severity of the disgust that is being communicated about those Christian women who refuse to cover their heads with a symbol of authority while performing spiritual functions.

NEXT PORTION OF THE TEXT

1 Corinthians 11:6
For if a woman does not cover her head, let her also have her hair cut off; but if it is disgraceful for a woman to have her hair cut off or her head shaved, let her cover her head.

It appears that Paul is using a form of sarcasm to make a cutting point. He's saying if a Christian woman refuses to cover her head and ornament herself with a physical covering to symbolize her station and authority, then she should be consistent with her decision to be a rebellious woman and just cut off her hair. Then he makes a statement addressing the obvious, "but if it is disgraceful for a woman to have her hair cut off or her head shaved, let her cover her head." In other words, Paul is asking for these women to be congruent in their logic. If you're a godly woman aiming to please the Lord by embracing your station in God's order and symbolizing your station and authority, then conform to this godly practice. But if you're a rebellious woman

---

[70] Charles Hodge. 1974. Commentary on Corinthians I and II. Edinburgh, Scotland: Banner of Truth Trust.

aiming to please yourself by disregarding your place in God's order of authority, then be consistent with your convictions and mark yourself as an insubordinate and disobedient woman by shaving your head.

Paul views the covering of men and the uncovering of women during spiritual activities of prayer and prophesying as a rebellion against God's design for spiritual authority. He associates this defiance with immense shame, implying the grievousness of a person unwilling to conform to this practice. In the next section, Paul continues to layer on further explanation for the doctrine of headship and anchors his argument of male and female authorities to the evidence seen in creation.

Chapter 07
AN ARGUMENT FROM CREATION

1 Corinthians 11:7-9

Providing a multi-dimensional defense is essential when presenting an argument, as it offers a more complete understanding of the topic at hand. Like describing a complex object, if you only give a one-dimensional view, it is limited and lacks clarity.

Adding dimensions provides a more nuanced understanding, and in the case of an argument, using multiple angles, perspectives, and sources of evidence can avoid oversimplification and misrepresentation. A multi-dimensional argument provides a more informed and persuasive case for a particular position, just as a multi-dimensional view of an object offers a more accurate and comprehensive understanding of it.

This is exactly what Paul is doing. He's already supported his claim for headcovering and uncovering by appealing to the divine structure of spiritual authority. Now, Paul anchors that spiritual authority by tying it to creation, resulting in a multifaceted and impenetrable argument.

THIS SECTION'S TEXT

1 Corinthians 11:7-9

For a man ought not to cover his head, since he is the image and glory of God, but woman is the glory of man. For man was not made from woman, but woman from man. Neither was man created for woman, but woman for man.

He starts this process in verse seven, saying, "For a man ought not to cover his head, since he is the image and glory of God." Pay attention to the word "since." This is called a causal clause. It could equally be translated as "because." Therefore, Paul is saying that the reason why a man should not cover his head while praying or prophesying is *because* he is "the image and glory of God."

This is not speaking only to husbands, fathers, single men, or pastors. This is teaching that all males who pray and prophesy must not cover their heads when they do so. He anchors the reasoning in their status and station as the "image and glory of God."

The same is true for women. This is not speaking to merely wives or mothers or girls. It's speaking to all females who pray and prophesy (girls, women, or wives). And the reason females are to cover their heads while performing these spiritual functions is because they are "the glory of man." Sadly, the translation committee for the ESV (English Standard Version) translation of the Bible has improperly interpreted the word γυνή (goonay) as "wife" when all other leading translations (KJV, NKJV, NASB, NIV, CSB, etc.) have translated it in its proper context as "woman."

Spiritual Authority and Being Under Authority

I want to make a vital and slight distinction. Man does not uncover his head because he's in submission to Christ, though he is. Man uncovers his head because he is "the image and glory of God." Likewise, Woman does not cover her head because she is in submission to Man, though she is. She covers her head because she is "the glory of man." The *root* reason for the coverings is not submission but to differentiate glories that relate to different degrees of authority. That said, the covering and uncovering *do* become visual aids and symbols for us that demonstrate submission, but the heart of this practice is to reflect the unique glories and authorities that were given to men and women. Dr. McFall explains this distinction well:

> "When she puts the covering of her own God-given authority (or power) on her head, she is acknowledging her station and position in God's authority structures. However, the covering must not be re-interpreted solely to remind her that she is under the headship of Man. That could give the covering a negative significance in the eyes of some, whereas Paul gives it a positive significance. The different

theological dress codes remind men and women of their place in God's order and the duties and privileges that go with that position."[71]

In other words, Woman is not without spiritual authority, she simply has a distinct spiritual authority—the spiritual authority of mankind. But what is the authority of mankind? In Genesis 1:28, God tells man *and* woman together, "Be fruitful and multiply and fill the earth and subdue it, and have dominion over the fish of the sea and over the birds of the heavens and over every living thing that moves on the earth." Dr. McFall comments, "All creation is subject to Eve (except Adam), and all creation is subject to Adam (including Eve)."[72]

I want to reiterate an important point about the distinction between women having authority and being under authority. In Matthew 8:9, we see an interesting statement from a Roman Centurion to Jesus. If you don't remember, this is the man with such great faith, he says to Jesus, "Lord, I am not worthy to have you come under my roof, but only say the word, and my servant will be healed." Then the Centurion says, "For I, too, am a man under authority, with soldiers under me. And I say to one, 'Go,' and he goes, and to another, 'Come,' and he comes, and to my servant, 'Do this,' and he does it."

The Centurion perceives what often goes unnoticed: that Jesus, like himself, is also subject to authority. And from submis-

---

[71] Dr. McFall, Good Order in the Church, Pg. 7–8.
[72] Dr. McFall, Good Order in the Church, Pg. 555.

sion to that authority, Jesus has incredible power. He has that power because He is in perfect submission to the source of all power—the Father. Likewise, for men and for women, submission produces authority.[73]

Under the Old Covenant and the structure of the Levitical priesthood, feminine authority in spiritual matters did not exist. But in Joel 2:28–29, the prophet says of the times after the cross, "And it shall come to pass afterward, that I will pour out my Spirit on all flesh; your sons and your daughters shall prophesy, your old men shall dream dreams, and your young men shall see visions. Even on the male and female servants in those days, I will pour out my Spirit." This passage is cited again in Acts 2:17–18. In our current New Testament age, women can place a symbol of authority upon their heads, the headcovering, and exercise their God-given authority to pray and proclaim the Gospel (prophesy). But there are boundaries. Women are not to exercise this authority over men, particularly in the spheres of family and church. But they can exercise this authority through evangelism and the edification of other women and children.

It is important to see that being in submission does not negate spiritual authority, it gives it. Not unmitigated authority but appropriate authority for that particular station. A Christian woman who is in submission to the male authority in her life (e.g., her father, husband, elders, etc.) is in submission to God, and from her willingness to fall in line with the divine structure

---

[73] This brilliant insight was derived from Dr. Finny Kuravilla's exposition of this verse that's available online.

of authority, through wearing a headcovering, she has been deputized by God to carry out the authority of her station. She can pray, prophesy, and rule over those areas within her jurisdiction. She is not without power, and she is not to be silenced or oppressed within her realm of power.

So, on the one hand, when a woman submits to the male headship figures in her life, she acknowledges her spiritual authority and is recognized as an obedient and humble woman who wisely uses the power she has been given. On the other hand, a woman who fails to submit to the male figures in her life throws off her spiritual authority and instead embraces prideful autonomy, rendering herself as an unauthorized woman who squanders her God-given power and rejects her station in God's order. Now, God knows which women are rebelling from ignorance and which women are rebelling from choice. But for those who are informed and still reject this divine order out of pride, should expect resistance from God who "opposes the proud but gives grace to the humble" (James. 4:6).

Unique Glories of Authority

If this book had a heart, this section is it. If we understand that God's directives for men and women serve a deeper purpose beyond religious practices, we can approach these commands with joy and willingly submit to their beauty. Let's look at our biblical text for this section once more before we move on.

THIS SECTION'S TEXT

1 Corinthians 11:7-9

For a man ought not to cover his head, since he is the image and glory of God, but woman is the glory of man. For man was not made from woman, but woman from man. Neither was man created for woman, but woman for man.

Glory Defined

To be glorious is to do what you were designed to do. Glory radiates from the one who rightly walks out their divinely appointed role. Hebrews 1:3 says of Jesus, "He is the radiance of the glory of God and the exact imprint of his nature, and he upholds the universe by the word of his power." Jesus is a radiant expression of God's glory because He is perfectly carrying out what He was designed to do, including perfect submission to the Father's will.

A glorious man is one who embodies manhood and submits to Christ, and lives and rules according to His will. A glorious wife is one who embodies womanhood and submits to her husband, and helps fulfill God's will in his life. A glorious child is one who obeys and honors his or her parents. A glorious meal is one that delights the tastebuds and satisfies hunger.

Adam and Eve are made in the image of God, but they have different glories. They are imaging different aspects of God. Adam's glory is imaged in the authority given to Him through creation order, and dominion. Eve's glory is imaged in submitting and helping Adam. Charles Hodge puts it this way, "Woman is not designed to reflect the glory of God as a ruler."[74] Eve's purpose was never to rule but to ornament and help her husband.

I once heard it explained this way: The woman is like the glory of the Moon. While she is made by the same Creator who made the Sun, her purpose is not to be the Sun but to reflect the Sun. The late theologian G.W. Knight says, "The Man reflects the One who directly created him, and thus, also, the Woman will inevitably reflect the one from whom she was created, namely Man."[75]

Another way to understand glory is to understand it as an expression of pride and joy. Later in 1 Corinthians 11:15, we will see that a woman's hair is a glory to her. That is, it is her pride and joy. Proverbs 20:29 says, "The glory of young men is their strength." In essence, their strength is their great possession. In 1 Thessalonians 2:20, Paul says to the Thessalonian Christians, "For you are our glory and joy." Dr. McFall speaks of this concept of glory being defined as pride and joy. He writes:

> "This captures what Man means to God: Man is God's pride and joy because of the direct, creational relationship that Man enjoys in God's world. Woman, on the other hand, is Man's pride and joy because of the direct, creational relationship that she enjoys in Man's world. Man was created

---

[74] Charles Hodge, Commentary on 1 Corinthians 11:7, Pg. 210.

[75] G.W. Knight. 1979. The Role Relation of Man and Woman and the Teaching/Ruling Functions in the Church. Chicago, IL: Journal of Evangelical Theological Society. https://www.etsjets.org/files/JETS-PDFs/18/18-2/18-2-pp081-091_JETS.pdf.

to relate directly to his Creator. Woman, on the other hand, was created to relate to Him through being related directly to Man. She brings glory to God by fulfilling her very specific Manward function. Man brings glory to God by fulfilling his very specific Godward function. He must be clear about why he is here on the earth, and likewise, she must be clear about why she is here on the earth. Their roles are completely different yet complementary under His headship."[76]

The Interplay Between Glory and Authority

To fully understand this passage, we must look to the creation account in Genesis. In Genesis 1:26, God says, "Let us make man in our image, after our likeness." In 1:27, it says that "God created man in his own image, in the image of God He created him; male and female He created them." This is important because Scripture confirms that Woman is, in every way, made in the image of God. However, our passage claims that Man is both the image *and* the glory of God, while Woman is the *glory of man*. That is, while Woman is the *image* of God, she is not the glory of God but the glory of man. Again, to be ultra clear here, this does not diminish the value of women whatsoever; it's merely a distinction between glories.

Men's and women's unique glories are derived from the unique stations of authority bestowed upon them by God. With regard to human authority within a family and church, man has been bestowed God's glory to be the head. He is to be a ruler like God.

---

[76] Dr. McFall. Good Order in the Church, Pg. 31.

However, his glory only comes from God (who is his authority). A woman has been bestowed with Man's glory (or the glory of mankind) to be above all other creatures and to subdue the earth by way of childbearing and helping her husband. Therefore, her glory comes not from God but from Man, from whom she was made and who is her earthy authority. Dr. McFall clarifies:

> "Adam was "the glory of God"—the finest thing He ever created. Adam was the apple of His eye: the one to whom He could delegate power and authority to rule the earth on His behalf and for His glory. That was his function; that was why he was made. Eve, on the other hand, was created not to fulfill Adam's role directly but indirectly through the specific task of being his helper. She had a different glory: she was created to be "the glory of man"—the finest thing Adam could possess."[77]

This does not mean that women do not also submit directly to God. Christ is the Head of all men, and through Man's headship, He is head of Woman, too. Therefore, it simply means Woman's submission regarding earthly matters in the family and the church comes through submission to her authority (or head) which is the Man who manifests as (her father, husband, church elders, etc.).

Now, submission must be defined. First, it has nothing to

---

[77] Dr. McFall. Good Order in the Church, Pg. 344.

do with superiority or inferiority. Submission is a willingness of a subject to accomplish the will of its head. Jesus says in John 5:20, "I can do nothing on my own ... for I seek not to please myself but him who sent me." Later in John 15:5, He says to His disciples, "I am the vine; you are the branches. Whoever abides in Me and I in him, he it is that bears much fruit, for apart from Me you can do nothing." Jesus submits perfectly to the Father, redeemed Man submits to Christ by the power of the Holy Spirit, and redeemed Woman also submits to Man by the power of the Holy Spirit. Essentially, you have Christ who says to His Head (God), "Not my will be done but yours." You have Man saying to his Head (Christ), "Not my will be done but yours." And you have Woman who says to her head (Man), "Not my will be done but yours."

While Woman's head is Man, that manship is manifested in a variety of roles: father, husband, brother, and church elder. These roles have varying degrees of biblical authority. For example, girls are to obey their fathers, and wives are to obey their husbands. But what about single Christian women? Is a woman directionless before she finds a husband? Of course not! She was made to be a help to Man and can certainly bless men (fathers, brothers, church elders, etc.) as long as she does so with appropriate decorum. Naturally, when she marries, her husband becomes the immediate manifestation of her head, and the help she can give to mankind, in general, is now channeled through one man in particular.[78]

---

[78] Dr. McFall. Good Order in the Church, Pg. 33 (Paraphrased).

While a single woman may be without a clear manifestation of a male head, she is never truly without a head. According to 1 Corinthians 11:3, Man (or menfolk) is her head. But does that mean she needs to submit, obey, and help all men? No. The better question becomes, how should Christian women relate to the male relationships in their life? Below are a few general principles I see in Scripture:

- An unmarried Christian woman with a Christian father would submit and serve the loving authority of her father (Eph. 6:1–4; Gen. 2:24). This would occur until her father gives over his authority to her husband as her immediate head.
- An unmarried Christian woman without a Christian father would honor her father but spiritually submit to the elders at her local church and serve her brothers in Christ (Heb. 13:17; 1 Pet. 5:5).
- A married Christian woman with a Christian or non-Christian husband would submit and serve her husband in all things that do not cause her to sin against God. (Eph. 5:22–24; 1 Pet. 3:1–22; Col. 3:18). He would be her immediate head and would remain so until either he or she died.

Again, this does not mean a woman does not submit directly to God—she does. Her submission in earthly matters, however, comes through submitting to her God-given head. The same is true for men. If a man attempts to come to God without submitting to Christ (his Head), he will not succeed. Paul says, "For there is one God, and there is one mediator between God and men, the man Christ Jesus." A woman cannot submit to God if she refuses to submit to the appropriate manifestations of her God-given head. Ultimately, I'm demonstrating that there is never a time when a Christian woman is without a head—because her head is Man.

Now, because a Woman's head (Man) can be sinful (even Christian men) there are limitations of his authority. If the men in her life are not walking under the authority of Christ (their Head), a woman must obey her head's Head (Christ). This requires discernment on the woman's part. For example, if a husband wants to move from Texas to California and the wife thinks it's irresponsible because her aging parents live in Texas, this is not a clear case for her to be insubordinate. However, if a husband asks his wife to lie for him about their taxes to keep him out of trouble with the law, she can refuse on the grounds of the ninth commandment. In other words, a woman is given the freedom of Peter and John in Acts 5:29 when the civil authorities commanded them to sin against God by not preaching the Gospel. Their response was, "We must obey God rather than men."

However, in a normal Christian family or church (sin included), this is the order of derived authority laid out by God and is a beautiful expression of God's way of ruling the world. When Christian men and women walk faithfully in this order, it produces a symphony of fruitfulness that radiates the rule of

God before an unruly world.

Edentic Foundations

While we, as New Testament Christians, have many passages that clearly teach about Man's authority and Woman's submission to that authority in the family and church (Eph. 5:23; 1 Tim. 2:11–15, 3:1–16; 1 Cor. 11:3; 1 Pet. 3:1; Tit. 1:5–9, 2:3–5; Col. 3:18), we must see how these passages find their substance by looking back to the God-given order of authority seen in the Garden of Eden. We can see this in five ways:

1. **Adam was created before Eve (Gen. 2:7).** Man and woman were not created simultaneously, but Man holds precedence as the firstborn in chronology. Furthermore, Man's existence did not require Woman. This is in contrast to Woman whose chief reason for existence (to help) was dependent upon the existence of Man.

2. **Adam was given God's glory to rule over all other creatures, including Eve (Gen. 3:16).** Adam was deputized by God to represent Him as a ruler and take dominion over creation. He was not subordinate to angels, archangels, or other spiritual authorities but had a direct and personal relationship with God.[79] More than that, Man was made biologically a ruler with an inclination to lead, govern, and

---

79 Dr. McFall. Good Order in the Church, Pg. 31 (Paraphrased)

control. God endowed Man with unique intrinsic faculties to be a proficient king over creation. However, God made it clear that Adam was not free to rule without Him.

3. **Adam alone was given the instructions for morality in the Garden, making him authoritative and responsible for Eve (Gen. 2:15–17).** God entered into a covenant of works with Adam before Eve was created, which he broke when he allowed Eve to lead him into sin. We see Adam's covenantal responsibility in three ways: First, in that, after sin entered into the world, God did not call Eve or them both to Himself, but called only for Adam (Gen. 3:9), who was the responsible party. Second, when it comes to their expulsion from the Garden, there is only mention of Adam, because, in his expulsion, Eve is included (Gen. 3:22–24).[80] Thirdly, Scripture demonstrates that Adam is held accountable for not only Eve's sin but the original sin of all people who come from him (Rom. 5:12; 1 Cor. 15:21–22).

4. **Adam was given Eve as a helper to him (Gen. 2:18–25).** There is no institution by which the helper exercises dominion over the leader. Even in the instance of the Holy Spirit's earthly ministry (who is called the Helper and is equally God), He comes to us by the sending of the Father and the Son (John 14:26). Namely, this is another example of submission among equals. Dr. McFall pointedly states,

---

80 Dr. McFall. Good Order in the Church, Pg. 6.

"Eve's purpose for living was determined by the pre-existence of Adam. She was to be a loving companion, wife, and mother." He adds, "Her origin arose from a sense of need that originated in Adam, not God."[81] Adam was alone, and God said of his aloneness, "It's not good." As a result, he creates a daughter and, as her Father, gives her away to Adam in marriage. Consequently, Woman was brought into a reality where God and Adam had already been in a relationship and where divine work was already assigned. Therefore, her design, physically, emotionally, and spiritually, was uniquely crafted to fulfill the specific needs of Man. Her very reason for existence was not to pave her own path beside Adam but solely to assist in the pre-existent, God-given work of Adam.

5. **Adam was granted the right to name Eve, demonstrating his authority over her (Gen. 2:23).** Eve answered to Adam, and he answered to God. In marriage, men still name their wives. For example, Ms. Abagail Johnson becomes Mrs. Abagail Smith. This act of a woman receiving the name of a man through marriage is still seen and resisted today. Nevertheless, the duty of naming is always carried out by a position of authority (e.g., a parent, owner, master, etc.). Moreover, in addition to Adam naming his wife "Eve" (Gen. 3:20), Adam also

---

81 Dr. McFall. Good Order in the Church, Pg. 10.

named her sex as "Woman" which literally means "out of man" (Gen. 2:23). This demonstrates that the principles of headship were not limited to Adam and Eve as individuals but extend to the male and female sex. That is, Adam's sex named the female sex. This was another important expression of God's design for male authority over the females within their jurisdiction (wives, daughters, sisters, etc.).

It's important to note that this structure was established in a world without sin. That is, God's design for male headship and female submission is not a result of the Fall. This is a freeing truth that should permit both men and women to rest in the holiness and goodness of God's design for the family and church.

After the Fall, this once holy, loving, and orderly relationship with God and Man and Man and Woman had been corrupted and disordered. The love that once kept these relationships pure had been distorted by sin. The only hope for a restoration of peace and harmony was for humanity to be reconciled to God. This is accomplished by Christ, who redeems us and restores love and order in the hearts of His people through the Holy Spirit. Jesus becomes the Second Adam, the Lord of all and the perfect Head of His bride—the Church.

Bruce Waltke, who wrote *The Role of Women in the Bible*, said, "In sum, the Bible is a story of Paradise lost in the first Adam and being regained in the Second. The Garden of Eden symbolically represents the ideal order that was lost and that Christ restores more perfectly in His church through the Spirit."[82]

Jesus, in His earthly ministry, upholds the creation order and gender roles set forth in the Garden (Matt. 19:4–6). But more than that, He perfects them as the second Adam. As Mediator between God and Man, He inserts Himself as Head of Man, producing accountability and modeling a loving relationship (1 Cor. 11:3). As this new and better Adam, He gives men the perfect example of what it means to be a loving authority (Eph. 5:25; Matt. 20:28, 1 Tim. 3:1–12). He does this most directly through His relationship with His bride—the new Eve—the Church. He gives men a pattern for right fatherhood, brotherhood, and even sonship. But He does not leave women without instruction. They are to be like the Church—the new and better Eve that comes from Christ in the same manner that Eve came from Adam. Tertullian spoke of this parallel when he wrote:

> "As Adam was a figure of Christ, Adam's sleep that produced Eve from His side was a shadow of the death of Christ and the wound inflicted on His side that produced the Church—the new Eve—the true mother of the living."[83]

Augustine affirms the same truth with different words:

---

[82] Bruce Waltke. 1992. "The Role of Women in Worship in the Old Testament." Ldolphin.org. 1992. http://www.ldolphin.org/waltke.html.

[83] Tertullian. 2018. A Treatise on the Soul. Lighthouse Publishing. (I modernized the language of this quote to increase readability).

"Adam sleeps that Eve may be formed; Christ dies that the Church may be formed. Eve is formed from the side of the sleeping Adam; the side of the dead Christ is pierced by the lance so that the Sacraments may flow out, of which the Church is formed. Is there anyone to whom it is not obvious that future events are represented by the things done then, since the Apostle says that Adam himself was the figure of Him that was to come?"[84]

Jesus does not introduce a new order for man and woman. He instructs men and women to adhere to a redeemed version of the order set forth at creation. In the perfect spiritual union of Christ and the Church, men and women can see and experience an expression of what Adam and Eve were intended to be.

Therefore, the Garden remains the reference point for right thinking around male and female relationships, authority, and glory. As we saw, Adam houses the glory of God in a unique way that Eve, and all women, do not. Again, the glory of God in Adam comes from God's authority vested uniquely into Adam. Adam, in a real sense, was the representative of God and was subordinate to God, who was his Head. Eve was the representative of Man and subordinate to Adam, her head.

In conclusion, Paul's purpose for referring to the creation account was to establish the reason for his instruction for head-

---

[84] St. Augustine. 1979. In Ioannis Evangelium Tractatus 9, 10; Translated by W. A. Jurgens, The Faith of the Early Fathers. Vol. 3. Collegeville, MN: Liturgical Press, 117.

coverings. The Garden of Eden is the foundational source for understanding the appropriate relationship between men and women, their respective authorities, and glories. The act of uncovering and covering the head during worship simply becomes God's chosen way to symbolize these important truths.

Glory and Spiritual Modesty

To fully understand the meaning of this passage, it is crucial to explore one final dimension of glory—radiance. This aspect of male and female glories is key to grasping the essence of the passage. Let's review this section's text once more:

> **THIS SECTION'S TEXT**
>
> **1 Corinthians 11:7-9**
> For a man ought not to cover his head, since he is the image and glory of God, but woman is the glory of man. For man was not made from woman, but woman from man. Neither was man created for woman, but woman for man.

I want to focus particularly on the phrase, "but woman is the glory of man." As we know, man has a particular glory as a representative of God. Woman has a particular glory as a representative of Mankind. In other words, men and women both radiate a particular glory and, according to Scripture, this glory radiates from the physical head.

First, we need to see our functions of worship (private or

corporate) as entering into heavenly courts. We are performing spiritual acts for the spiritual world. For that reason, God's glory takes precedence above all other glories. In Revelation 4:10–11, we see a glimpse of heavenly worship. The passage reads:

Revelation 4:10–11
The twenty-four elders will fall down before Him who sits on the throne, and will worship Him who lives forever and ever, and will cast their crowns before the throne, saying, 'Worthy are You, our Lord and our God, to receive glory and honor and power; for You created all things, and because of Your will they existed, and were created.'

First, it is worth noting that the elders in Revelation 4, who are not angels, remove their crowns before praising God. While it may seem like a stretch to consider a crown to be a headcovering, it is important to remember that Paul's instruction does not prohibit the use of a specific type of headcovering. Rather, it forbids *any* object on the physical head of a man during worship. 1 Corinthians 11:4 says, "Every man who has something on his head while praying or prophesying disgraces his head." Thus, the act of casting their crowns aligns with the doctrine of headcoverings.

Second, see that worship, at its core, is the glorification of God. The elders say, "Worthy are You, our Lord and our God, to receive glory and honor and power…" Namely, the essential purpose of worship is to ascribe glory to God.

As we know, Man is the glory of God. Therefore his glory is not to be covered during functions of worship as God's glory should not be hidden. However, Woman does not radiate the glory of God, but the *glory of Man* and mankind should not glory in the presence of God. Therefore, during all functions of worship, God's glory should not be rivaled by Man's glory. Namely, mankind's glory, the Woman, should be covered when God's glory alone should be seen. So while the matter of head-covering and uncovering is certainly about physical practices representing authority and headship, it's equally about spiritual modesty by moderating the appropriate glories at the appropriate times.

The seriousness of worshiping covered as a man or uncovered as a woman cannot be ignored. It is a matter of reverence. At the very least, a disregard for this practice would be disrespectful, and, at the very most, it would be blasphemous.

NEXT PORTION OF THE TEXT

1 Corinthians 11:8-9

For man was not made from woman, but woman from man. Neither was man created for woman, but woman for man."

Man was made *for* God and *from* God, while Woman was made *for* Man and *from* Man. (Adam's rib, see Gen. 2:22–24). In 397 A.D., the great early church scholar Ambrose of Milan spoke about the origin of Woman and her relationship to Man by showing a parallel to the origin of the church and its relationship to Christ. He says, "Women are commanded to be subject to men by the law of nature because that man is the author or beginner of the woman; for as Christ is head of the church, so is Man of the Woman, from Christ the church took beginning, and therefore it is subject unto Him; even so, did Woman take beginning from Man that she should be subject."[85]

This does not mean that a woman cannot give God glory. She certainly can and must! As I said earlier, she was made equally in His image for His glory (Is. 43:7; Eph. 2:10; 1 Cor. 6:20, 10:31). God's design for headship simply teaches that woman glorifies God most by doing what she was designed to do—to help Man fulfill God's will. Yes, she is to have her own devotion to the Lord. Yes, she is to obey the commandments. Yes, she is to worship her Creator. But her primary earthly *ministry* is to help and complement Man. This can be a hard concept for a feminized and individualistic society to accept. But when men and women resign themselves to their God-given identities, they can rest in their unique glories and honor God before the world.

The Fusion of Symbols and Principles

In recent years, some commentators have accepted the principle of headcoverings but changed its application. For example, John MacArthur says of this passage, "It is the principle of women's

---

[85] St. Ambrose. 2018. Exposition of the Christian Faith. Iv.28.32; Paradise Iv.24, x.28. Lighthouse Publishing., and in his First Epistle to Timothy, as quoted by Marvin A. Breslow, The Political Writings of John Knox (Washington: The Folger Shakespeare Library/ London and Toronto: Associated University Presses, 1996), p. 51.

subordination to men, not the particular mark or symbol of that subordination, that Paul is teaching in this passage. The Apostle is not laying down a universal principle that Christian women should always worship with their heads covered."[86] John MacArthur and others like Dr. Daniel Wallace make the argument that wedding rings or modest clothing are sufficient symbols to fulfill Paul's command.

As someone who was trained on how to interpret Scripture at John MacArthur's seminary, I find this to be a strange and wildly inconsistent interpretation. It is never okay to divorce a principle from its symbol. For example, Baptism is both a principle and a symbol. The principle is the remission or cleansing of sins, and the symbol is water that washes us. To change the symbol from water to, say, a gust of wind that drives away dirt would not be okay. Another example is The Lord's Supper. The principle of the Lord's Supper is the reconciliation of a person to God through the body and blood of Jesus Christ. The symbols are bread and wine. To change those symbols to steak and soda would be an unthinkable heresy.

Bruce Waltke, in his commentary on this passage, said, "The picture of His rule must not be seized by believers into their own hands to shape it according to their own pleasure. In 2 Kings, 16:10–11, Ahaz incurred the wrath of God by changing

---

[86] John MacArthur. 2023. "Head Coverings for Women." Grace to You. January 24, 2023. https://www.gty.org/library/bibleqnas-library/QA0219/head-coverings-for-women.

the shape of the altar to conform it to Assyrian demands."[87]

We are not free to reconstruct the symbols that God has chosen to represent His truths. When humans can change sacred symbols, the intended meaning of that biblical symbol will soon be lost. More importantly, the symbol becomes inconsistent throughout the church, causing confusion and making unity on the matter impossible.

Glory from the Head

It is important to understand the biblical and historical connection between glory and the head. Throughout Scripture, bodily glory is generally associated with the face, which is a portion of the head. Here are several biblical examples:

- In Exodus 33:18–23, we see that the pinnacle of God's glory is in His face. The text says, "Then Moses said, 'I pray You, show me Your glory!' And He said, 'I Myself will make all My goodness pass before you, and will proclaim the name of the Lord before you; and I will be gracious to whom I will be gracious, and will show compassion on whom I will show compassion.' But He said, 'You cannot see My face, for no man can see Me and live!' Then the Lord said, 'Behold, there is a place by Me, and you shall stand there on the rock; and it will come about, while

---

[87] Bruce K. Waltke, ed. 1978. 1 Corinthians 11:2–16: An Interpretation by Bruce K. Waltke. Vol. BSAC 135. Bibliotheca Sacra. https://www.scribd.com/document/220628251/Waltke-1Corinthians-11-2-16-an-Interpretation.

My glory is passing by, that I will put you in the cleft of the rock and cover you with My hand until I have passed by. Then I will take My hand away, and you shall see My back, but My face shall not be seen."

- Jesus, who is the radiance of the glory of God (Heb. 1:3), affirms the same focal point of glory in His transfiguration in Matthew 17:1–2. It says, "And after six days Jesus took with him Peter and James, and John, his brother, and led them up a high mountain by themselves. And he was transfigured before them, and his face shone like the sun, and his clothes became white as light."
- In 2 Corinthians 4:6, Paul tells us, "For God, who said, "Let light shine out of darkness," has shone in our hearts to give the light of the knowledge of the glory of God in the face of Jesus Christ."
- In Revelation 1:16, the face of Christ is again shown as the illuminating portion of his being. It says, "In his right hand he held seven stars, from his mouth came a sharp two-edged sword, and his face was like the sun shining in full strength."
- In Exodus 34:29–35, we see that after Moses speaks with the Lord, he returns, radiating the glory of God in his face.
- In Numbers 6:25, the Lord commands Aaron to tell the Israelites, "The Lord make his face to shine upon you and be gracious to you;"
- In Isaiah 6:1–2, we see that even the Seraphim cover their faces in the presence of God's glory.

- In Acts 6:15, we see that during Stephen's proclamation of the Gospel, his face is illuminated. It says, "And gazing at him, all who sat in the council saw that his face was like the face of an angel."

There is a clear connection between glory and the human face in Scripture. The face, as we know, is merely a portion of the head. Anatomically, you cannot separate the face from the head. This connection is not only understood logically but seen creatively throughout church history. For example, halos have been used throughout church history to signify glory and radiance around the heads of those deemed "holy."

Now, by sharing these passages of Scripture, my intention is not to argue that 1 Corinthians 11:2–16 mandates women to veil their faces, but to highlight a crucial biblical principle regarding the general location of glory on the human body. As per the biblical standpoint, glory is attributed to the head and not any other section, such as the chest, arms, or legs. Therefore, my aim is to point out the odd determination to redistribute this symbol of headship away from the head.

For example, Dr. Roy B. Zuck, in his book, ironically titled *Basic Bible Interpretation*, says of headcoverings, "Should women today wear shawls on their heads in church? No, because the significance of women wearing shawls in the Greco-Roman world no longer holds true in our culture. The act does not carry the symbolism it once had. But is there a principle here to be followed and to be expressed in a modern-day cultural equiva-

112 A COVER FOR GLORY

lent? A possible modern cultural parallel, some have suggested, is the wife's wedding ring (and changing her last name to that of her husband) which shows that she is married and thus is under her husband's authority."[88]

This argument for the wedding ring fails for several reasons. First, wedding rings are not gender specific. That is, both men and women commonly wear wedding rings. However, when it comes to headcoverings, Paul gives distinct instructions to men and women. According to 1 Corinthians 11:4, men who pray or prophesy with their heads covered dishonor their head (Christ). Therefore, if we were to assume that wedding rings could be a substitute for headcoverings, it would imply that men are not permitted to wear wedding rings, when they pray or prophesy, which is clearly not the case. Second, wedding rings were practiced before 1 Corinthians was written, so if Paul had rings in view, he would have used wedding rings and not headcoverings.[89] Third, wedding rings are symbols of love and covenant, not symbols of authority. Lastly, the doctrine of headcoverings is not about marriage; it's about the distinction of authority and glory between Man and Woman.

God has given us head symbols to signify headship.[90] He

---

88 Roy B. Zuck. 2013. Basic Bible Interpretation. Colorado Springs, CO: David C Cook Publishing Company.

89 Sebesta, J., & Bonfante, L. (2001). The World of Roman Costume (1st ed., p. 78). Madison, Wis.: University of Wisconsin Press / See also: Hersch, K. (2010). The Roman Wedding (1st ed., p. 41). Cambridge: Cambridge University Press.

90 Jeremy Gardiner. 2017. "Can Wedding Rings Replace Head Covering?" The Head Covering Movement. March 28, 2017. https://www.headcoveringmovement.com/articles/can-wedding-rings-replace-head-covering.

did not give us hand symbols or feet symbols. The passage clearly and repeatedly speaks of headship, and it is sensible that God would institute symbols for our heads to communicate those principles.

To believe that we can replace or relocate biblically assigned symbols for the head to other locations of the body is not only bad interpretation but also a prideful and dangerous way to approach Scripture.

Inconsistency of Interpretation

As we have seen, Paul argues for the practice of headcovering from the truths that are seen in creation. Interestingly, the only other time in the New Testament that Paul anchors an argument in creation to validate his doctrine is in 1 Timothy 2:11–14 on the topic of women teaching in the church. The text says:

> **1 Timothy 2:11–14**
> Let a woman learn quietly with all submissiveness. I do not permit a woman to teach or to exercise authority over a man; rather, she is to remain quiet. For Adam was formed first, then Eve; and Adam was not deceived, but the woman was deceived and became a transgressor.

I find it fascinating that many conservative Christian pastors hold firmly to this doctrine of not permitting a woman to have authority in the church and do so by demonstrating how Paul connects his command to the creation order. This is interesting because they are willing to use the two verses in 1 Timothy, which anchor the prohibition of woman pastors to the truths of creation, but they are not willing to use the three verses from 1 Corinthians 11:7–9, which anchor the purpose of headcoverings to the principles of creation.

Rachel Held Evans, who recently died, was a popular feminist theologian and saw this interpretive inconsistency between these two passages. She writes in an essay:

> "Anyone who says that Paul's instructions regarding the women at Ephesus are universally binding because he appeals to the creation narrative to make his point can be consistent in that position only if they also require women in their church to cover their heads, as Paul uses a very similar line of argumentation to advocate that."[91]

This is certainly an inconsistency of interpretation, and even liberal commentators can see it. Having said that, I also adhere to the prohibition of women teachers and pastors in the church. Not only is the creation argument for headcovering more dense and robust than that of the prohibition of women teaching but, as we will see, the headcovering argument is anchored further in the spiritual realm, human nature, and universal church practice.

So what's really happening? How are these pastors who have proven themselves capable of strong expositional work

---

[91] Rachel Held Evans. 2012. "For the Sake of the Gospel, Let Women Speak." June 7, 2012. https://rachelheldevans.com/blog/mutuality-let-women-speak.

still denying this doctrine of headcoverings? I have a theory—feminism is powerful. More significant and impactful than our comprehension can fathom.

The Force of Feminism

Just as the ocean current can carry you further from the shore without you realizing it, so too can the influence of feminism subtly guide a pastor's beliefs and practices until they are far removed from the firm foundation of God's Word. Allow me to provide a few examples.

First, the feminist movement has caused pastors (even strong pastors) to fear women. In fact, many pastors fear the women in the church more than they fear the men. This is not without reason. Today's feminism has militarized women, including Christian women, and made them more aggressive, manipulative, and divisive than ever before. An article titled *When Men Fear Women*, which hosts a featured image of a medieval painting of a woman on a horse trampling a brigade of men, demonstrates this without reservation. The article opens, "It's good to make men feel fear, and this is something women absolutely have the power to do."[92] This warlike tone is not uncommon today. Consequently, men have grown increasingly afraid to offend women in an effort to not "poke the bear." This is why you get catchphrases from husbands like, "I've got to check with the boss," or more generalized phrases like "happy wife, happy life." Women have become intimidating to

---

92 Leah Finnegan. 2017. "When Men Fear Women." The Outline. October 24, 2017. https://theoutline.com/post/2421/when-men-fear-women.

many men. As a result, women largely have become the unpastored community of the church. They are the untouchables. You can see this in the difference between Mother's Day and Father's Day sermons. On Mother's Day, the pastor tends to shower praise and adoration on mothers. On Father's Day, the sermons are more likely to present a critical and demanding message full of expectations and areas for improvement. Although it may seem like a minor instance, the pattern of modern pastors demonstrating partiality is a troubling concern.

When it comes to teaching on a practice like headcoverings or women pastors, many preachers truly fear the backlash and disruption that would come with a faithful exposition. As a result, they don't teach on it, or they hold to some strange interpretive inconsistency as a way to side-step the issue. It really does take a bold pastor to teach on headcoverings, willing to possibly lose a portion of his church, to teach the women in his congregation that the Bible calls them to symbolize the very thing many Christian women hate—submission to Man.

Second, over the years, I've watched more and more pastors buy into the psychotherapy fallacy that a person cannot speak about what they have not experienced. In other words, experience becomes the authority for teaching rather than Scripture. As a result, men are disqualified from speaking about women's issues because they are, of course, not women. Therefore, in a church with a male pastor, women again become the untaught community of the church. Yes, they hear doctrine and theology, but how often do you hear male pastors do a series or class on wifehood, motherhood, or women's sins? The fear of being called a "mansplainer" is high.

Our experience is not our authority; Scripture is our authority. This is why I can speak to adultery without being an adulterer. I don't need to cheat on my wife to speak to those who have cheated on their wives. According to Scripture, I have *less* authority if I am speaking into the same sin which I am committing (Matt. 7:5).

Third, men love women. This is good, but when we overextend or modify the truth of Scripture to demonstrate our love for women, that is wrong. Pastors all over the modern world look at this text and see the perceived social and emotional difficulties, embarrassment, or shame that headcoverings might cause for a woman. Out of a false sense of mercy, these pastors refrain from taking the passage literally.

Fourth, men want to be liked by women. If maintaining a good reputation among the women in your church requires you not to deliver them the truth, you're more concerned with pleasing women than pleasing God. In the case of headcoverings, no pastor wants to be labeled as a misogynist, but that is certainly the title they will receive from some if they hold to the clear doctrine of headcoverings. Mary Kassian, who wrote *The Feminist Mistake* speaks to this elusive influence feminism has made on pastors:

> "We are entering into an era in which feminist precepts are largely accepted by default. This has profound implications

for the evangelical church. In the past, the feminist agenda was pursued by a small but radical group of theologians devoted to the cause. But now the agenda is being furthered by pastors and theologians who would not consider themselves feminists at all and who would, in fact, be quite aghast to be labeled as such. However, I believe that those who adopt feminist philosophy—even unwittingly—are placing themselves on the side of a divide that will lead far away from the Christianity of the Bible."[93]

We cannot overlook the influence that feminism has had upon pastors, their exegesis, and their preaching. Culturally speaking, feminism is in the air we breathe and the water we drink. The impact it has made on the church is immense. The unlearning and relearning required for a realignment with Scripture is significant. Therefore, Christian men and women must be willing to throw off our modern and easily offended sensibilities and ruthlessly question our practices against the teaching of Scripture. When Scripture becomes the church's standard and cornerstone, then we will finally begin to restore the gender-role dysphoria of our day.

Concluding the Creation-Based Argument

The practice of headcovering and uncovering during spiritual functions is a symbol of the divine structure of spiritual authority

---

[93] Mary A. Kassian. 2000. The Feminist Mistake: The Radical Impact of Feminism on Church and Culture. Wheaton, IL: Crossway Books.

and the distinction of glory between Man and Woman. This distinction is not about superiority or inferiority but rather about reflecting the unique glories and authorities that were given to each gender. The Garden remains the reference point for right thinking and principles around male and female relationships, authority, and glory. While feminism has had a significant impact on the modern church, a realignment with Scripture will help us restore the gender-role dysphoria of our day. Therefore, it is crucial that we uphold these sacred symbols (uncovering and covering) that God has chosen to represent His truths, so that the meaning behind those symbols will not be lost and unity on the matter can once again be achieved in the church.

Chapter 08

AN ARGUMENT FROM THE SPIRITUAL REALM

1 Corinthians 11:10

"Therefore the woman ought to have a symbol of authority on her head, because of the angels."

I remember my old Sunday school teacher would always say, "Whenever you see the word 'therefore,' you must ask 'What's it there for?'" In other words, "therefore" is a signal word. It's demonstrating cause and effect.

It's another way of saying "on that ground," or "consequently," or "as a result." You could quite literally translate this verse to say, "*As a result*, the woman ought to have a symbol of authority on her head." In other words, the Apostle is saying, "I have proved by creation that Woman is made in the image of God but subordinate to Man and hosting a different glory as it pertains to authority. *As a result*, it is clear that the Woman is to display her submission and moderate her particular glory by covering her hair and/or head during spiritual activities."

Where people get thrown for a loop is the causal clause in the next phrase, "because of the angels." This phrase has produced some outlandish ideas by those who do not understand the text. But, as you will see, this is not all that difficult to interpret.

In our day and age, it's not uncommon to see physical symbols that help spectators visually distinguish authority. There is a reason a police officer does not dress the same as a civilian. His uniform demonstrates he is a man under the authority of the local government to carry out a particular duty. More precisely, his badge becomes the most potent symbol of his station and the role he must play as a result. In the passage above, the Apostle argues that a woman ought to cover her head not only for the earthly observers who are edified by her willingness to accept her station as a woman under authority but also for the sake of the spiritual observers—the angels.

The Scriptures teach about the unique presence of angels (righteous and fallen) and, therefore, this passage most likely refers to the edification of the angels who, by watching over the saints, can see which women were under the authority of Christ (by way of Man) (see Heb. 1:14; Matt.18:10; 1 Pet. 1:12). If the angelic realm (including the demonic) has such a great involvement and interest in the spiritual matters of men, we should not be shocked by their attendance of our worship of God when in private or in the Lord's Day assembly. Furthermore, whenever we are aware of the presence of higher authorities, it always produces better behavior. The Apostle is likely alluding to this effect by assuring us that we are being watched not only by God but by the inhabitants of Heaven.[94] A secondary view that is probable but

---

94 Joseph Agar Beet. 1882. A Commentary on St. Paul's Epistles to the Corinthi-

less direct may be speaking to the respecting of the angels who, while in the presence of God's glory, also covered their glory (by covering their heads) in Isaiah 6:2.

Symbols of Reverent Order

As mentioned earlier, when we worship on earth, we join the ongoing and neverending angelic worship that occurs in heaven (Rev. 4:8, 5:12; Is. 6:1–2). As we know, the angelic world knows the facts of mankind. In addition, they know their station in relation to mankind. Namely, mankind is one step lower than the angels in God's divine arrangement (Heb. 2:7, 9). Certainly, they understand the doctrine in our passage that states that Christ is the head of Man and Man is the head of Woman. That is, they fully comprehend the realities behind creation order and unique glories and authorities. Angels understand that Woman is not to rule and take authority over Man (1 Tim. 2:12). Therefore, when joining them in heavenly worship, they undoubtedly are concerned with how we partake. Our glories should be properly moderated with men uncovered, and women covered.

William Mouser, in an essay titled *Hair and Worship* writes, "And so, it is for the women to have a mark of authority on her head, because of the angels, creatures whose worship we join, singing along with them in our worship, whose angelic sensibilities of propriety and rank are shocked in a worship service where any glory but God's is improperly on display."[95] In other

---

ans. London: Hodder and Stoughton. Paraphrased, Pg. 184.

95 William Mouser. 2007. "Hair and Worship." Archive.org. 2007. https://web.

words, when a woman wears a headcovering, she maintains proper decorum during worship, honoring the angel's own understanding and ensuring that God's glory is the only glory on display. The 19th-century English theologian Robert Knight adds:

> "God has given to man and woman different kinds of authority, and the outward and visible token of these is represented in a covered head for Woman (to represent her God-given authority), and an uncovered head for Man (to represent his God-given authority). If a Man covers his head in the presence of the angels (in the ecclesia, or formal gathering of the Church), it signals that he has only the authority allocated to Woman. This is not glorifying to Christ, his Head, who gave him authority belonging to Man. Similarly, if a woman uncovers her head, she is declaring (by her uncovered head) that she has the authority given to Man. This is not glorifying to Christ either, because she is female. She is declaring that she is equal to Man. This is going against the created order of authority. She has been given her own authority, and she should be content to live within that ordained sphere and not grasp for authority that God has not given to her."[96]

We must understand that the spiritual functions of prayer and prophecy go beyond physical actions and are also observed and

---

archive.org/web/20150715060616/http://fiveaspects.net/hair-and-worship/.

96 Robert Knight. "Paul's Rebuke of Women Praying with Uncovered Heads: A New Interpretation of 1 Corinthians, Chap. XI. 10," Journal of Sacred Literature 4 (July, 1849) 88–101.

heard in the spiritual world. Therefore, when women wear head-coverings during worship, they not only symbolize their submission to God's design for gender roles and authority to fellow human beings but also to the angelic realm, where the distinct glories and authorities of Man and Woman are also recognized.

THIS SECTION'S TEXT

1 Corinthians 11:10

Therefore the woman ought to have a symbol of authority on her head, because of the angels.

A Covering for Two Worlds

To understand this passage further, we must first understand God's intention for a woman's hair. Not only does Scripture say that her hair is a glory to her (1 Cor. 11:15), but it also implies that it covers her shame (baldness; see 1 Cor. 11:5–6). As we all know, this is not true of men. Hair is never said to be or explained as a glory for a man. In fact, some women prefer men with bald heads. Additionally, men experience significantly less shame about baldness than women. Dr. McFall says:

> "God, the wise Designer, planted a dread in every woman to avoid appearing in public without her covering of hair, and this instinct goes back to the drawing board stage of her design. Paul notes that just as God has covered her physical baldness (i.e., her shame) with a physical covering of hair to hide it, and this covering makes her acceptable and "normal"

in the physical world, so the artificial covering has a mirror function in the spiritual world and makes her acceptable and "normal" in the eyes of the multitude of onlooking and ministering angels. What her natural covering of hair does for her in the physical world of men, the artificial cover does for her in the spiritual world of the angels."[97]

Ultimately, women need to be adorned in two different spheres—physical and spiritual. Physical baldness and spiritual baldness (uncovered) are equally shameful to two different audiences—men and angels. To the men, a bald woman is unpleasant because her glory has been removed. To the angels, an uncovered woman is unpleasant because she improperly worships in the spiritual appearance of Man. Paul attempts to make this connection between being uncovered and being bald in 1 Corinthians 11:5, which says, "But every woman who has her head uncovered while praying or prophesying disgraces her head, for she is one and the same as the woman whose head is shaved." We live in a time when baldness among women has become "trendy" or even "fashionable." It is only those things because it is rebellious against the traditional standards of God's design. We also live in a time when society celebrates ugliness. This is not how Christian women are to think and define beauty. A woman's hair truly is a distinguishing feature that identifies her as a woman. It is the focal point of her glory and physical beauty and is celebrated by God, Man, and angels. If Christian women grasped the signifi-

---

[97] Dr. McFall. Good Order in the Church. Pg. 334.

cance of their hair, they would cherish it, guard it, and moderate it according to God's standards of modesty.

Chapter 09

MEN AND WOMEN EQUAL BEFORE GOD

1 Corinthians 11:11-12

"However, in the Lord, neither is woman independent of man, nor is man independent of woman. For as the woman originates from the man, so also the man has his birth through the woman; and all things originate from God."

A few years ago, I was gifted a beautiful heirloom goatskin Bible from a company called Schuyler. On the cover in the bottom right corner, in gold foiling, is "Romans 11:36." That verse says, "For from him and through him and to him are all things. To him be glory forever. Amen."

It's my favorite verse in the Bible because it reminds me that all things come from God. Paul understands what happens when people forget this truth. In this verse, Paul addresses the sin of exploitation and guards against men abusing this gifted position of authority. He reminds the church that while God has dispensed a higher degree of authority to Man and the role of submission to Woman, they are both mutually dependent upon one another. In fact, we cannot exist without each other. Dr. McFall writes:

"We might sum up the position in the couplet, "Equal in worth; unequal from birth." "Equal in worth" refers to the price God paid to redeem women as well as men. They both need His Son's blood to redeem them. "Unequal from birth" refers to the fact that God made male and female, and made one subject to the other's love, care, and authority. Their roles cannot be reversed. The roles are gender-specific, fixed, and set in theological concrete."[98]

This mutual dependence should demonstrate that while the authority is patriarchal, the physical, emotional, and spiritual relationship is complimentary. No man can rightfully claim he has no need of a woman, and no woman can rightfully claim she has no need of a man. God has, in His perfect wisdom, designed this union to spur on mutual Christlikeness. Man's strength, discernment, and logic are of great value to Woman, and Woman's nurture, tenderness, and support are priceless to Man.

    I can attest to the incalculable value of women in my own experience with my wife and daughter. I often tell young Christian men who are courting a woman that if I could have grasped what I know now of my wife (her love and value to me) during our days of dating, I would have married her the first day we met. Veronica's contribution to my life and ministry is immeasurable. A similar sentiment is held regarding my daughter, who, at the time of this writing, is only nine. However, even at such a young age, she has greatly supported me. In fact, it has been my prayer to

---

[98] Dr. McFall, Good Order in the Church, Pg. 322.

have more girls. The Lord, however, has chosen to give me three more boys instead, so I'll keep praying.

John Calvin made a similar statement regarding his wife Idelette after her death in 1549. He wrote, "I have been bereaved of the best companion of my life, of one who, had it been so ordered, would not only have been the willing sharer of my exile and poverty but even of my death. During her life, she was the faithful helper of my ministry. From her I never experienced the slightest hindrance."[99]

This value of a woman is not only demonstrated in marriage but in parenthood—especially motherhood. Paul states that "Man has his birth through Woman." The indebtedness of a man to his mother should never be forgotten as he, as a child, was fully dependent upon her for survival. So while men may have authority over women, they must not wield that authority with negligence to the gratitude they owe to them for their nurture.

While Woman comes from Man in creation, Man comes from Woman through birth, but all comes from God. Paul directs our eyes from creaturely production back up to divine production. God is the Author of it all—the male-female idea, the order of events seen in creation, the authorities and glories that were distributed, and the relationships between them. For this reason, all we have learned in this passage is good because it all finds its origin in the mind of a holy and all-wise God.

Ultimately, even though headcoverings symbolize the

---

[99] Philip Schaff.. 2012. History of the Christian Church, Volume 8 Modern Christianity the Swiss Reformation. Rarebooksclub.com.

distinctions of authorities and glories between men and women, Paul wants to emphasize that these distinctions should not create division by making one sex feel superior or inferior as they both equally come from God.

Chapter 10

AN ARGUMENT FROM NATURE

1 Corinthians 11:13-15

Imagine standing on top of a mountain, gazing out at a vast and sweeping landscape. While the view is awe-inspiring, you quickly realize that the distance can obscure hidden details and features.

But as you descend the mountain and explore the terrain up close, hidden details become visible, offering a more comprehensive understanding of the landscape. By examining the terrain in detail, from its broad contours to its individual features, you gain a nuanced understanding that cannot be achieved from a distance.

Similarly, when trying to understand an issue like headcoverings, it is important to be able to zoom in and zoom out, moving between the big picture and the details. As we can see, Paul takes us back to the issue of hair to observe the finer implications for our discussion.

THIS SECTION'S TEXT

1 Corinthians 11:13-15

Judge for yourselves: is it proper for a woman to pray to God with her head uncovered? Does not even nature itself teach you that if a man has long hair, it is a dishonor to him, but if a woman has long hair, it is a glory to her? For her hair is given to her for a covering.

Paul opens with the words, "Judge for yourselves." This is not Paul offering permission to the Corinthians to judge if what he was writing was true. This is his appeal to the Corinthians' own sense of decorum or religious etiquette. It is a call to examine their own conscience. He uses this same tactic to prove the obvious in 1 Corinthians 10:15–16. Interestingly, this appeal to self-examination has more power than you might think. I cannot tell you how many women my wife and I have met over the years who, prior to fully grasping the doctrine of this passage, had a strong conviction in their conscience to cover their heads while performing spiritual functions. It was, in some way, a doctrine embedded in their very being. Namely, they had an intrinsic proclivity toward spiritual modesty but had never heard the clear teaching on headcoverings.

Paul goes on to support his appeal to their conscience with the testimony of nature. The word "nature" does not refer to the animal kingdom or wildlife but to the nature of Man and Woman. If I could paraphrase, Paul is saying something like, "Isn't it obvious? Doesn't even the natural biologies of Man and Woman demonstrate this truth of uncovering and covering? Look, God has made man appear glorious with short hair and woman appear glorious with long hair. Isn't this correct in your own observation? Doesn't a man look shameful when he looks like a woman, and a woman looks shameful when she looks like a man?"

As I have already pointed out, it's hard to see this basic truth because men and women have lost a sense of shame as it pertains to hairstyles. We have men running around with man-buns and women with boy cuts dyed blue. When Paul refers to natural hair length, I believe he's also talking about how men and women of every tribe, nation, tongue, and era have acknowledged, from native instinct, that a man's hair is to be short and a woman's hair is to be long. Yes, there are exceptions to this truth, but they are rare. History, art, archaeology, and literature all attest to the normative practice of men having shorter hair and women having longer hair. Length, however, is relative. For example, in biblical times, a man may have had shoulder-length hair, but women of that same era had hair reaching to their lower back. That is, the distinction between male and female lengths has always been present in varying degrees around the world.

In an article by Time Magazine titled *How Did Long Hair Become a Thing for Women?* Merill Fabry discusses the history of hair. She writes:

> "Though hair fashions may change season to season, the association between women and long hair is an ancient one. It dates back at least to ancient Greeks and Romans, and

according to archaeologist Elizabeth Bartman, even despite the Ancient Greek ideal of a "bearded, long-haired philosopher," women in that society still had longer hair than men regularly did. Roman women kept their hair long and tended to part it down the center, and a man devoting too much attention to his hair "risked scorn for appearing effeminate."[100]

Kurt Stenn, who has over 30 years of expertise studying hair as a Distinguished Professor of Pathology and Dermatology at Yale University, wrote in his book *Hair: A Human History*, says, "It is almost universally culturally found that women have longer hair than men." He continues to say, "In order to have long hair, you have to have your needs in life taken care of."[101] Namely, long hair was both time-consuming and expensive. But more than that, long hair was a nuisance that would obstruct manual labor. Long hair held in more heat, increased sweat, could be caught on surrounding materials and was not functional for hardworking men.

Ultimately, Paul calls them to observe the evidence of biology and sociology. His aim is to demonstrate that these agree with what he is saying, and rejecting his teaching is accepting incongruity with both their conscience and mankind's nature.

A Glory to Her

In verse 15, Paul states that a woman's hair is a "glory to her." As

---

[100] Merrill Fabry. 2016. "Now You Know: How Did Long Hair Become a Thing for Women?" Time, June 16, 2016. https://time.com/4348252/history-long-hair/.

[101] Kurt S. Stenn. 2017. Hair - A Human History. New York, NY: Pegasus Books.

a being, she is the glory of Man. But as a woman, her hair is her glory. So, if Man is the radiance of God and Woman is the radiance of mankind, then her hair is the pinnacle of feminine glory. It is the apex of her beauty, and it is what makes her appear womanly. This undebated fact is evidenced by the intrinsic attraction men have to women with long hair.

The Mishnah (old rabbinical writings on the Law) made it clear that a woman untying her hair in public was an extreme act of immodesty. In an article titled "Religious Hair" in *Studies of the New Testament*, the author said, "The person injured when a married woman uncovered her hair in public was her husband, who was put to shame. He had a right to his wife's hair being covered in public."[102] In other words, to that culture, long, flowing, uncovered hair was today's equivalent of a wife wearing a bikini to a public beach. She became eye candy for lustful men. I mention this historical perspective to help remind us how captivating a woman's hair can be. I am not saying Scripture teaches us that a woman's hair must be covered at all times as a form of sexual modesty. I do, however, want you to know that a woman's hair can certainly contribute to the sexual attraction of men. Now in a time where we're our culture struggles to see why wearing leggings and a low-cut top to church is wrong, this sexualized view of hair will likely be seen as extreme and outrageous. But the fact that hair can be sexual is proven across modern media. In fact, *Glamour*

---

102 Derrett, J. Duncan M. 1977. Studies in the New Testament, Volume 1 Glimpses of the Legal and Social Presuppositions of the Authors. Article: Religious Hair. Leiden, Netherlands: Brill.

Magazine cited a study performed by Pantene (a woman's hair product company) that concluded with some incredible truths:

- 74% of men indicated that they notice women because of their hair, and 44% of men surveyed said that hair is the first thing they notice about a woman, more than her clothes (26%), legs (25%), or makeup (4%).
- Most men surveyed would be more likely to approach a woman at a bar with great hair than a woman wearing a low-cut shirt.
- 82% of men indicated that sexy hair is a key element to a woman's overall sex appeal.
- 60% of men surveyed say they would rather date a woman with great hair than a woman with big breasts.
- And 78% of men surveyed consider healthy hair to be a turn-on.[103]

What this study tells us is that a woman's hair can be very arousing and distracting to a man. This does not negate his need for self-control, but no godly woman should aim to attract the eyes of men during the worship of God (1 Tim. 2:9; 1 Pet. 3:3–4). Therefore, during public acts of spiritual functions (praying or prophesying), the headcovering becomes a tool of modesty for the godly woman. In a real sense, it puts her in control to cover

---

103 Beth Shapouri. 2011. "Want to Know What Men Really Notice When It Comes to Your Hair? Check out These Survey Results." Glamour. February 9, 2011. https://www.glamour.com/story/want-to-know-what-men-really-n.

AN ARGUMENT FROM NATURE 141

her own beauty and to eliminate the all-too-often wandering eyes of men. She can prohibit her glory from being a stumbling block for her brothers in Christ. Dr. McFall cites Antoinette Clark Wire, who wrote *The Corinthian Women Prophets*, and explains her position this way:

> "The covering served another incidental (but maybe not unintentional) purpose: it covered the woman's glory, her hair, her beauty, her power to attract men. This God-given power to attract men continues to operate after she is married. Her beauty continues to fascinate single and married men at all times and places. In the world, it is a constant threat to every marriage: it cannot be turned off. The covering of her head, to some extent, lessens her unwitting power to attract/distract the attention of men during the most important function that men can ever enter into—the worship of God Almighty. Nothing should distract the worshippers from this duty. Her hair is her glory, and this is not to be immodestly displayed in the worship service."[104/105]

Scripture does not limit a woman's glory (her hair) to be seen in common Christian life. There is freedom under the Gospel to celebrate this God-given glory when it is presented with the ethics of elegance and modesty. A woman can present her glory

---

[104] Dr. McFall. Good Order in the Church, Pg. 200.

[105] Antoinette Clark Wire. The Corinthian Women Prophets: A Reconstruction Through Paul's Rhetoric. United States, Wipf and Stock, 2003.

freely in times and places that will not cause men to stumble or draw away their focus from the glory of God, who is our focus.

Hair as the Covering

The phrase, "For her hair is given to her for a covering," has many people say, "Boom! It's right there—the hair is the covering. Case closed! Headcoverings are not needed; let's move on."

However, of all the arguments against headcoverings, this may be the weakest of them all. How? Because in 11:6, Paul says, "For if a woman does not cover her head, let her also have her hair cut off; but if it is disgraceful for a woman to have her hair cut off or her head shaved, let her cover her head."

In other words, if the hair is viewed as a headcovering, why would Paul say, "For if a woman does not cover her head, let her also have her hair cut off"? Just slow down for a moment to look at this with me. If her hair is the covering, then you must read the text like this:

> "For if a woman **does not cover her head with hair**, let her also have her hair cut off…"

This interpretation of the text creates a logical contradiction within the passage, revealing that the covering that Paul is referring to is not a woman's hair.

Furthermore, the fact that Paul only commands covering for women during certain functions (praying or prophesying) is also evidence that he is instructing the use of a removable covering.

Because if the hair were the covering he has in view, they would always be covered during *all* functions (because women don't take off their hair). More importantly, if the hair is the covering that Paul is calling for, why would Paul even have to write to tell women to cover their heads? Again, are women in the habit of taking off their hair? What would that even mean? Under the view that hair is the covering, it would be like Paul writing to tell women to wear their hands when they pray and prophesy. Of course they are going to wear their hands; their hands (like their hair) are connected to their body!

Some scholars have argued that Paul said this because of the great number of Corinthians prostitutes in the city. The primary source quoted comes from the ancient Greek geographer Strabo (64/63 B.C.–24 A.D.). His work *Geographica*, which was written about 30–40 years before 1 Corinthians, documented that in Corinth, "The temple of Aphrodite was so rich that it owned more than a thousand temple slaves, courtesans, whom both men and women had dedicated to the goddess."[106] These scholars escape the jurisdiction of this entire doctrine on headcoverings by claiming this passage was written with these prostitutes in mind. However, this is injecting circumstances into the text that do not appear in the passage. R. C. Sproul says of those who adopt this view:

> "If Paul merely told women in Corinth to cover their heads and gave no rationale for such instruction, we would be

---

106 Strabo and United States Congress House. 2013. Strabonis Geographica. Rarebooksclub.com.

strongly inclined to supply it via our cultural knowledge. In this case, however, Paul provides a rationale which is based on an appeal to creation not to the custom of Corinthian harlots. ... We must be careful not to let our zeal for knowledge of the culture obscure what is actually said."[107]

Paul does not reference local customs but the unchanging order of creation, the testimony of nature, the presence of angels, and, as we will see, the official teaching of the apostles and universal adoption of all churches. These factors solidify that this teaching on headcoverings is not subject to cultural norms and are therefore applicable in all settings and in all eras.

Hair as the Covering and the Original Greek

Paul is calling for an artificial covering. It makes no sense for the Apostle to write a 15-verse argument telling women to cover their heads with hair that already covered their heads. That said, I want to deal with a few less common arguments presented primarily by those who have experience in the original Greek. This is important because, at some point, you will bump into someone who will attempt to disprove this entire doctrine with an argument from Greek grammar.

Below, I will present three Greek grammatical issues to demonstrate that a woman's hair is not a sufficient covering:

---

[107] R.C. Sproul. 2016. Knowing Scripture. Downers Grove, IL: Inter-Varsity Press.

1. Covers his head

To prove that Paul is talking about an artificial cloth covering, we need to clearly see that the word "covering" in our passage means "an artificial covering." Let's start by looking back at 1 Corinthians 11:4, which says, "Every man who has something on his head while praying or prophesying disgraces his head." The phrase "something on his head" in Greek is "κατά κεφαλης" (*kata kephalēs*).

The only other place in the entire Bible where this exact phrase is used is in Esther 6:12 in the Septuagint (the third-century B.C. Greek translation of the Old Testament). For those of you who know the story of Esther, Haman had planned to sabotage Esther's uncle Mordecai, but the king had become aware of his scheme, and Haman is now forced to honor Mordecai in public. In verse 12, it says, "Then Mordecai returned to the king's gate. But Haman hurried home, mourning, with his head covered." The phrase "his head covered" is "kata kephalēs" (the same exact wording in 1 Corinthians 11:4).

The question we must ask ourselves is this: Was the author of Esther telling us that Haman hurried home with his hair on? No, Haman was ashamed and embarrassed and grabbed a cloak or a piece of fabric and hid himself under it. That is, we see the phrase "*kata kephalēs*" is not talking about hair as the covering, but an artificial covering.

Another instance is found in secular Greek literature by the first-century Greek philosopher Plutarch. He said in an essay on the Roman General Scipio, "As he [Scipio] came to Alexandria and landed, he went with *his head covered*, and the Alexandrians running about him entreated he would gratify them by uncovering and showing them his desirable face. When he uncovered his head, they clapped their hands with a loud acclamation."[108]

Again, our exact phrase "*kata kephalēs*" appears and is further evidence that hair is not the covering but that Paul is referring to but to an artificial cloth covering that goes over the head.[109]

2. For a covering

In English, 1 Corinthians 11:15c says, "For her hair is given to her for a covering." For those of you who know Greek, it reads, "Ὅτι ἡ κόμη ἀντὶ περιβολαίου δέδοται."

I would like to look at the word "περιβολαῖον" (*peribolaion*), which is the noun "covering" in "for a covering." In our entire passage, the root word used for "cover," "covered," or "uncovered" is "κατακαλύπτω" (*katakaluptó*), which means "to cover." Which we know is an artificial covering. But in the phrase "For her hair is given to her *for a covering*," Paul uses a completely different word! He uses the word "περιβολαῖον" which means "something thrown around one." It gives the image of a shawl being thrown around a woman's head. In the first five instances, Paul is clearly talking about an artificial covering. But when he argues that even

---

108 Plutarch. 1874. Plutarch's Morals Translated from the Greek by Several Hands. Corrected and Revised by. William W. Goodwin, PH. D. Boston. Little, Brown, and Company. Cambridge: UK: Cambridge Press Of John Wilson and Son.

109 Dr. Finny Kuravilla does an excellent job explaining this in his three-part YouTube video series on headcoverings.

nature demonstrates the principle of a covering, he uses this new word. It could be translated as this: "For her hair is given to her as a beautiful shawl." Paul is making the point that even nature demonstrates that long hair is glorious on a woman and, for this reason, she has been given, by God, this beautiful shawl of hair. This is an important distinction as it will help us in the following argument.

3. "For a covering" or "in place of a covering"

Our final word study is "ἀντὶ," (which is also translated in the New Testament as "instead," "upon," "as," and "because." Some critics of headcoverings argue that the correct translation is "instead," causing the English to say, "For her hair is given to her *instead* of a covering."

Dr. Bryan Findlayson, who wrote *Exegetical Study Notes on the Greek New Testament*, says, "By using the word "ἀντὶ," [Paul is] expressing "equivalent to" = "for," rather than substitution, "replaced by." He explains by saying, "Of course, if a woman's hair is a God-given covering for her head, why does she have to wear another covering? Paul's analogy simply serves to make the point that "nature" (the way things are) provides a woman with a covering, and this supports Paul's instruction that a woman should cover her head. Nature has given Woman hair as a glorious and natural cover. Therefore, women should follow the lead of nature, as defined by worship decorum, and cover their heads."[110]

---

110 Rev. Bryan Findlayson. n.d. "Exegetical Commentary on 1 Corinthians 11:2–16." Lectionarystudies.com. Christian Ministry Resources. Accessed February 23,

The Greek exegetical scholar A. T. Robertson adds by saying, "The phrase "ἀντὶ περιβολαίου" does not mean "in the place of a covering," but is comparing the physical covering with the natural covering. He provides a congruent example by saying, "In John 1:16, it says, "καὶ χάριν ἀντὶ χάριτος" (in English: "and grace *for* grace")."[111]

Therefore, the word "ἀντὶ" does not refer to a replacement but to a type of equivalent. John is not saying, "and this grace instead of that grace." No, he's saying, "and this type of grace upon that type of grace." He's demonstrating two graces that are different but equal. They are layers of grace. Now, as it pertains to our verse, Paul is showing how the natural hair is an equal but different type of covering. This makes sense because Paul used a new word for covering in this verse. Had he used the same word as the previous five instances, there would be no reason to demonstrate equality because they are the same word. However, because Paul used "περιβολαὶον" (*peribolaion*) instead of "κατακαλύπτω" (*katakaluptó*), he needed to demonstrate equivalence.

What is being taught here is that the hair in the natural arena is what the covering is in the religious arena. Equal but different. It is one covering answering another covering. Therefore the preposition, in context, is a preposition of comparison, not substitution. Practically speaking, Paul is showing the similarity between the two, since they are two different words. When in

---

2023. http://www.lectionarystudies.com/studyn/epiphany1epfen.html.

111 A.T. Robertson. 1982. Word Pictures in the New Testament. 1 Corinthians, Vol. 1 11:15. Ada, OK: Revell.

worship, there is a covering that prevents her from spiritual shame. When in the worldly arena, there is the long hair that prevents her from earthly shame. In other words, there is no place, spiritual or natural, where a woman should be uncovered. If she is bald or uncovered during worship, it is shameful and absent of her God-given glory.[112]

Now, I know this might have been difficult to follow, but I wanted to show you the reason every major Bible translation (NASB, ESV, KJV, NKJV, CSB, and NIV) has translated this phrase as "for a covering" or "as a covering" and not "instead of a covering."

The takeaway lesson is this: If the equal but different covering (her hair) is a glory to a woman, then her glory should not be glorying in the presence of God's glory. Therefore, she should have an additional and artificial covering over her hair (her glory) during all forms of spiritual worship, corporate and private.

---

112 Ignatius, Mar David. n.d. "Bishop's Epistle." Blogspot.com. Accessed February 23, 2023. http://bishopjerrylhayes.blogspot.com/2020/07/in-quote-from-modern-cinema-particular.html. (Paraphrased).

Chapter 11

AN ARGUMENT FROM THE CHURCH

1 Corinthians 11:16
"But if one is inclined to be contentious, we have no other practice, nor have the churches of God."

Suppose you are walking down a busy street in a large city. You see a group of people gathered on the corner, all looking up at something in the sky. As you approach, you realize that they are all pointing at a hot air balloon that is floating overhead.

At first, you may be skeptical. You may wonder if the balloon is really there or if it is just a trick of the light. But as you look around, you realize that everyone else on the street is also looking up at the balloon. In fact, the vast majority of people around you are pointing and staring at the balloon. The fact that so many people are pointing at the balloon makes it much more likely that the balloon is really there. You may still have doubts or questions, but the fact that so many other people are seeing the same thing gives you a certain level of confidence that you are not alone in your observation.

Similarly, in an argument, the fact that a majority of people hold a particular view can be a powerful indicator of the strength of that view. Especially when that view is backed by logic, fact, or sources that have proven trustworthy. Ultimately, consensus suggests that the view has been tested and validated by a large number of people, and that it is not just the opinion of a few individuals.

This is Paul's approach in his final defense. Having now reasoned from authority, creation, the spiritual realm, and nature, Paul makes his final argument from the practices of the Apostles and the universal Christian Church.

You can see Paul's confidence in how he opens this section, "But if one is inclined to be contentious." That is, he's saying if anyone disagrees with the extensive argument I have just put forth, "we have no other practice." In other words, if a person rejected Paul's argument, this was the position of all the Apostles. Namely, Paul doesn't simply provide a sufficient set of arguments but also leverages the authority of the other Apostles to give his words additional force and persuasive power.

Although it may be tempting to assume that women are the contentious ones, based on my experience, both men and women exhibit equal levels of contention. As I mentioned in earlier chapters, the cultural practice of the day was in exact opposition to Paul's instructions. The men were the ones who would wear headcoverings during worship, and women would generally not. Paul could have surely anticipated objections from either sex.

If a person rejects the arguments of the text and the authority of the Apostles, Paul makes one last appeal by leveraging the testimony of the universal Christian church. That is, if words don't convince you, maybe sociological evidence in the church will.

No Such Custom

Some of you might be reading a translation that says, "no such practice" or "no such custom" instead of the NASB95 (that I'm using), which says, "no other practice." It's possible that in the letter the Corinthians wrote to Paul (which we don't have), they presented to Paul what they believed to be a "Christian custom" or their "Corinthian custom" that was contrary to Paul's teaching here in Scripture. The Apostle is then clarifying that they (the Apostles), who were sent by the authority of Christ, have no such custom other than what Paul just explained. Namely, according to the Apostles, there is no Christian custom or church that permits men to pray and prophesy covered or women to pray and prophesy uncovered. Dr. McFall says:

> "The introduction of an ancient, non-apostolic custom is not worth discussing," Paul tells the Corinthians. "Forget it. We have our own theological traditions. Don't replace them." Paul's appeal to apostolic tradition justifies an appeal to Early Church tradition where it agrees with Scripture and with apostolic practices."[113]

Paul's final appeal to the church is to clarify the customs of the

---

113 Dr. McFall. Good Order in the Church, Pg. 338

Kingdom of God. Any rejection of this practice would be deviant to the Christian dress code. Paul appeals to the people of God here extensively. You cannot find many other topics of Scripture where Paul puts together such a thorough explanation. As a result, we can say with confidence that this doctrine of headcoverings is the universal practice of the Christian Church.

Section Three

CONCLUSION AND APPLICATION

Chapter 12

CONCLUSION:
EMBRACING DISTINCTIONS

Pastor Brian Sauvé once said, "Every worldview has a uniform."[112] We can see this truth clearly displayed in how the feminists dress—the short hair, the masculine style, the baggy clothing, tattoos, and their overall look of androgyny.

For gay men, it's the exact opposite. They begin wearing tighter clothing, amplify their grooming, wear more feminine colors and jewelry, and some even add makeup. In other words, it's unarguable that people modify their dress to symbolize their sexual and gender ethics. A person's dress tells their story and reveals their worldview. This concept is not foreign to God. In the Old Testament, God introduced various dress codes to His people. From the priests to the average person, God distinguished

---

112 Brian Sauvé, Lexy Sauvé. 2023. Bright Hearth: What About Head Coverings? New Christendom Press. https://podcasts.apple.com/us/podcast/what-about-head-coverings/id1616730798?i=1000599283561.

his people in various ways. But these distinctions were not only between the Israelites and other nations they were also between men and women.

In Deuteronomy 22:5, we read, "A woman shall not wear a man's garment, nor shall a man put on a woman's cloak, for whoever does these things is an abomination to the LORD your God."

Headcoverings are, in a real way, the means for telling God's story and God's doctrine through the dress of His people. To God, a man worshiping with his head covered and a woman worshiping with her head uncovered is a sight of spiritual transgenderism, and it is shameful. It is shameful because it removes the visual distinctions that uphold God's order among His people. More than that, when God's people throw off this Kingdom custom, it no longer acts as a beacon of structure to a sexually confused and disordered world. Therefore, this practice of headcoverings has both internal and external effects. The internal effects are related to our relationship with God, the angels, and one another in the local church, while the external effects are related to the world's view of the Church and the Church's work in the world.

Internal Effects

I often tell my children, "We are the beneficiaries of obedience to God." In other words, God does not create certain practices and rules for His advantage but for ours. Because the practice of headcoverings is directly linked to the foundational truths of Man and Woman, this practice offers both males and females deep

CONCLUSION: EMBRACING DISTINCTIONS

anchors of identity, clarity, and rest. When we know who we are, why we are here, and what we are made to do, it offers us a settled sense of relationship with God, the opposite sex, and ourselves.

Furthermore, this practice of headcoverings gives us explicit instructions for honor and shame. Dr. McFall says:

> "'Every man who prays and prophesies with his head covered dishonors his head, that is, he dishonors the Lord Jesus before God and the angels. And similarly, in the case of an uncovered woman's head, 'who prays and prophesies with her head uncovered dishonors her head,' that is, she dishonors Man in general and her husband in particular (if she is married), in the presence of God, Christ, and the angels.'"[114]

The internal effect of this practice is honor. Honor to God. Honor to Christ. Honor to Man. To believe that we can worship and pray in honor while deliberately ignoring God's instructions for honorable worship is nothing short of pride. Are we to be described as the fools in Proverbs who "Do what seems right in their own eyes?" Are we to enter the heavenly courts with a practice of shame? Are we to petition God in a posture of disgrace? Of course not! John 4:24 tells us, "God is spirit, and those who worship him must worship in spirit and truth." For that reason, we do not come to the King, ignoring the customs of the Kingdom. The doctrine of headcoverings is clear. They are a custom that is honoring to God and is good for us.

---

[114] Dr. McFall. Good Order in the Church, Pg. 310.

What we cannot forget is this: Rebellion prohibits blessing. In 2 Kings 5:1–14, we see the story of Naaman the Leper and the prophet Elisha. Naaman was too proud to obey God's word and "Go and wash in the Jordan seven times" that he would be healed. His disobedience prohibited his blessing. The same is true of the one who knows God's customs for prayer and worship yet fails to conform to them. That person puts off the blessings of God.

What we have learned from 1 Corinthians 11:2–16 is that our appearance before God matters to Him. Today's casual culture that shows up on Sunday in a t-shirt and jeans has eaten away at the concept of showing reverence with dress. As I stated earlier, Christians will modify their clothing for business and banquets but not for worship. We must see that God is worthy of our outward modification. We must see that in this practice of headcoverings, He has instituted a timeless dress code that symbolizes His order for Man and Woman. Instead of opposing it, let us commemorate and demonstrate to a disordered and confused world the wisdom of our God.

As we know, this practice of headcoverings is, by and large, absent from half of the modern church. That is, generally speaking, this practice is *not* disobeyed by Christian men. More specifically, our churches are *not* filled with men covering their heads during worship. It is Christian *women* who are predominately not obeying this biblical practice. However, I would argue the failure of the women sits squarely upon the shoulders of men. Pastors, fathers, and husbands have either been passive, willfully ignorant or have not adequately interpreted this passage on headcoverings,

CONCLUSION: EMBRACING DISTINCTIONS

resulting in a lack of obedience from Christian women.

Collectively, this will be no easy tide to turn. Christian women, by and large, have been so desensitized by our egalitarian culture that the idea of marking themselves as subordinate to Man is viewed as some form of religious oppression. But obedience often comes before perfect understanding. In fact, I've learned that we understand through obedience. When it comes to more challenging commands, I ask myself, "Has Christ not earned my obedience? Is He not worthy of my change? Is His will not deserving of my conformity? Is His way not better than mine?" Asking these questions always softens my heart and prepares me to obey.

In other words, we must adhere to the biblical ethic of self-examination (1 Cor. 11:28; 2 Cor. 13:5; 2 Pet. 1:10–11). With regard to headcoverings, ladies, look deep within your heart. Are you resistant because you're not convinced by Scripture, or is your flesh fighting this command? If it's the latter, ask yourself, "Am I humiliated to identify with God's ways? Am I insulted by the station God has given me? Is biblical femininity weak in my eyes?" These are important inquiries surrounding this particular issue.

When I have fought similar battles with my own flesh, I am reminded of the words of our Lord, "You shall love the Lord your God with all your heart and with all your soul and with all your mind. This is the great and first commandment." In other words, if true love is sacrificial, then God commands total sacrifice from us. Namely, there is no cause of Christ unworthy of our complete and total submission. His ways are good whether we understand them or not. His ways are good even when others disagree. But most of all, His ways are good even when they cost us.

External Effects

As we know, gender identity is the crisis of our day. Our ministry's bestselling book is strangely a children's book titled *Jesus and My Gender* (dealing with biblical gender for kids). It is a book that would have been completely unnecessary 50 years ago. But here we are in the midst of an entire Western civilization that is perplexed by basic truths on fundamental issues.

All of this confusion, and I mean *all* of it, stems from a rebellion of God's design for males and females. We cannot be so naive to think that the church's deportation of headcoverings, God's symbols for masculinity and femininity, over the past 60 years has not, at least, partially been responsible for the West's growing pandemic of gender confusion. As we know, the Church is the light of the world and a city on a hill (Matt. 5:14–16). We are the pillar and ground of the truth (1 Tim. 3:15). We are representatives of the Kingdom (1 Pet. 2:9). Christians alone behold the knowledge of what is right and wrong regarding the issues of gender and sexuality, and we must never squander our influence before the world.

Unfortunately, I see many Christians buying into the world's thinking regarding these issues. That is, they acquiesce to the idea that homosexuality and transgenderism are merely social or civil issues or even "mental health" issues. They are not. They are biblical

CONCLUSION: EMBRACING DISTINCTIONS

issues. It is the Bible that tells us God created them male and female (Gen. 1:27). It is the Bible that condemns cross-dressing (Deut. 22:5). It is the Bible that forbids homosexuality (Lev. 18:22; 1 Cor. 6:9–11; Rom. 1:26–27; Jude 1:7; 1 Tim, 1:10). These are not social or civil issues, they are Christian issues.

The same can be said about feminism and the church. If we evaluate their movement by its own self-appointed mission of "sexual equality," it quickly reveals itself as an enemy of God. Males and females are not sexually equal. Yes, we are equally sinful, and we are equally redeemable, but we are unequal in biology, authority, responsibility, and function. While these distinctions have absolutely been lost in the world, they are being rapidly diminished within the modern church as well.

At the moment, the war is on the pastorate. Thousands of women are assuming positions of ecclesiastical authority. They have become pastors, elders, preachers, and teachers. An October 2018 report by the "Rev." Eileen R. Campbell-Reed found that in 2016, 20.7% of U.S. professional clergy were women, up from 2.3% in 1960.[115] According to a recent Barna study, 79% of Americans are comfortable with a female pastor, and 72.8% of evangelicals are fine with a woman preaching on Sunday morning.[116]

---

115 Anna Oakes. 2020. "Amid Growth in Leadership, One-Fifth of U.S. Clergy Are Female." Watauga Democrat. March 1, 2020. https://www.wataugademocrat.com/community/amid-growth-in-leadership-one-fifth-of-u-s-clergy-are-female/article_739b14a1-212a-5d06-b429-4d888a369255.html.

116 What Americans Think about Women in Power." n.d. Barna Group. Accessed February 23, 2023. https://www.barna.com/research/americans-think-women-power/.

In the end, we cannot deny the connection between doing away with headcoverings in the 1960s and the growth in the ordination of women—they are inextricably linked. When the symbols of authority are eliminated, the qualifications for authority are forgotten.

Elisabeth Elliot says of this issue, "The Church must choose between the ordination and the subordination of women. Which does God command? If subordination is the command of God, ordination is excluded. It is a contradiction."[117]

To choose incorrectly on this matter is costly not only to the Church but also to its witness to the world. For we know, as God's children, disobedience always results in judgment. This is clearly seen in the seven churches of Revelation as well as the chronicles of Israel. For example, In Isaiah 3, we see God's judgment upon His people for their disobedience. He says, "As for My people, children are their oppressors, and women rule over them." In other words, when God's people disobeyed, He punished them with disordered authority. Dr. McFall says:

> "For old Israel, the outward sign of spiritual decline—of God's judgment—was when women ruled over them. When they saw women in authority, they could conclude that all was not well with the nation's worship. The remedy was not to oust the women from positions of authority, but to repent and return to the Lord who would reset the nation on its feet

[117] Christianity Today. 1976. Vol. 20. Christianity Today.

CONCLUSION: EMBRACING DISTINCTIONS

again, and restore the judge and prophet to lead them."[118]

We certainly can see a similar judgment on the Western Church today. Our denominations are an ocean of disorder. As I demonstrated above, thousands of churches are currently ruled by women. And this is no small movement, either. The United Church of Christ, The Assemblies of God, The Methodist Church, The Evangelical Lutheran Church in America, some sects of the Presbyterian Church, and many others have all formally affirmed the ordination of women.[119] Hundreds more have become tolerant of the ideals of feminism and are increasingly looking for ways to accommodate these beliefs into their congregations.

Women are not designed to lead in the local church (or family), and when they do, disorder is the result (1 Tim. 2:11–12; 1 Cor. 14:34–35). More concerning, when the church affirms gender disorder at large (as we are seeing now), the world loses its reference point for what is normal and furthers the confusion even more. As of today, the Western Church is similar to defiant Israel, plagued with disordered leadership by God's judgment. It is only when Christians repent and recommit themselves to the doctrine of biblical headship (the doctrine which headcoverings symbolize) that we will begin to see a restoration of God's gender order among His people.

---

118 Dr. McFall. Good Order in the Church, Pg. 364

119 Michael Gryboski. 2021. "Women's History Month: 7 Christian Denominations That Voted to Allow Female Ordination." The Christian Post. March 7, 2021. https://www.christianpost.com/news/7-christian-denominations-that-allow-women-to-be-ordained.html.

The Path Forward

Gender distinctions are for our benefit. They are God's means to remind His people (and the world) of the spiritual truths and order they represent. When these truths are forgotten, chaos ensues. When these truths are remembered, order is established.

The path forward is actually quite simple. It starts with loving God. Jerry Bridges once wrote, "There is no question that obedience to God's commands, prompted by fear or merit-seeking, is not true obedience. The only obedience acceptable to God is constrained and impelled by love. God's Law, as revealed in His Word, prescribes our duty, but love provides the correct motive for obedience. We obey God's law, not to be loved, but because we are loved in Christ."[120]

That is, all true obedience must come from Gospel love. Love because Christ kept the Law that you couldn't keep. Love because Christ paid the eternal penalty you deserved. Love because you were, of God's sovereign will, chosen, spiritually resurrected, granted repentance, gifted faith, and imputed the righteousness of Christ. When this is in view, no command of Scripture is too great.

Therefore, as it pertains to headcoverings, the path forward requires nothing more than saved men and women who will throw off the influences of the world and obey Scripture no matter what. This will restore biblical masculinity and femininity. This will teach future generations God's order for authority. This will produce blessings in the church. But most of all, this will show the world how good and wise our God really is.

---

[120] Jerry Bridges. 2017. Transforming Grace. Navpress Publishing Group, 92.

Appendix A

IMPORTANT QUESTIONS, QUICK ANSWERS

Are headcoverings just for wives or all females?

The practice of headcoverings is not rooted in marriage; it's rooted in the particular authority that was given to all males and all females. The different authorities are what is being symbolized in this practice. Namely, the practice, at its core, is not about submission. For example, men do not uncover their heads to symbolize their submission to Christ. 1 Corinthians 11:7 says, "For a man ought not to have his head covered, since he is the *image and glory of God*." On the other hand, a woman does not cover her head to demonstrate her submission to her husband. She does so because "...the woman is the *glory of man*." In other words, this practice is about the distinctions between genders, their respective glories, and their God-given authorities. Therefore, all praying and prophesying males and females should uphold this practice of headcoverings.

How much of my head should be covered?

As we know, the passage does not give us direct dimensions. But it does give us the object for which is to be covered—the head—and, more particularly, the glory of a woman's hair. Unfortunately, the shame and embarrassment that many women experience when they cover have caused them to find smaller and smaller covers. From the outside, their "cover" is really just a headband or three-inch doily pinned to the back of a bun. So, at the basic level, the passage does use the word "cover." Now, if you bought a cover for your car and you pulled it out of the packaging, and it only covered the hood, could it still be considered a car cover? Probably not. The same logic applies to the head cover. My wife aims to cover the majority of her hair. In the Winter, she will wear a headscarf or shawl (similar to what you see on the cover of this book), and in the Summer, more of a head wrap covering the bulk of her hair. Her favorite retailer is GarlandsofGrace.com.

How often should I wear my headcovering?

The text is pretty clear; you are to cover and uncover (for men) when you pray or prophesy. Namely, whenever you partake in spiritual functions, a woman should cover her head. This would include times of private prayer and worship, family worship, evangelism, and the Sunday gathering. Now, there are some pitfalls that can cause this practice to become legalistic. For example, some ladies wear a covering all the time because they say, "Well, we're supposed to pray without ceasing." That's fine to say (and do) as long as it doesn't become a hard and fast rule for others. Additionally, other ladies think God won't hear their prayers if they don't cover. Rest assured, God hears the male construction worker's prayer even though he cannot remove his hard hat on the job. He also hears the prayer of the woman who forgot her covering at home. Ultimately, God looks at the heart and can rightly weigh the circumstances to determine if the issue is spiritual laziness or genuine impracticability.

What should I do if my husband disagrees with my conviction to cover my head?

Headcovering is intended to be an honor to a husband. Unfortunately, this practice can be a sensitive issue, and it's not uncommon for husbands to struggle with it. If your husband is unsure about headcovering, consider gently inviting him to investigate this doctrine (maybe by reading this book). If he's still not convinced, respectfully communicate your understanding and convictions. In a circumstance where headcoverings are firmly rejected, it is important to bear in mind that while wives are called to submit to their husbands, there are limits when it comes to following God's Word. If a husband disagrees with Scripture, a wife should prioritize obedience to God. That being said, consider the principle found in 1 Peter 3:1–2, which encourages wives to show respect and submission to their husbands, even if they are not following God's word. By doing so, their conduct and character may have a powerful impact on their husband's heart. In other words, on issues like this, a wife ought to lean more on the discipline of prayer rather than intellectual persuasion.

Should I leave my church if they don't practice headcovering?
There are lots of valid reasons to leave a church today—the tolerance of homosexuality, the preaching of a prosperity gospel, the ordaining of women, and the failure to preach clear and accurate biblical doctrine. But if your church has abstained from these areas of failure and upholds a biblical Gospel of grace, has strong expository preaching, and has scripturally qualified elders and deacons but doesn't believe in the practice of headcoverings, I suggest you stay. Better yet, as other women begin to ask you why you cover your head, share with them the truth of this doctrine or consider buying a few copies of this book to give away.

How can I humbly share the doctrine of headcoverings with others?
Whenever we hold a new doctrinal conviction, it is important to remember the journey God led us on to reach that conclusion. If you regularly wear a headcovering, it is natural for other women to be curious about it. In my experience, it is best to wait for them to ask and then share your personal testimony. However, it is even more important to guide them through 1 Corinthians 11:2–16. Be prepared to address common objections, such as those regarding local customs, hair as the covering, or the tendency to replace the symbol with something else. Above all, be patient with other women and offer them helpful resources such as articles and videos to navigate this issue wisely. I have included all my resources in the bibliography, but for specific resources that were especially helpful to me, please see the section titled "Special Thanks."

If headcovering is a practice for today, why wasn't it a practice under the Old Covenant?

In the Old Covenant, Man's head was God (not Christ), and the relationship was mediated by priests. These priests had a required dress code. Under the New Covenant, God introduced a new structure of headship for His people, with the introduction of God the Son as a Mediator *between* God and Man. In His infinite wisdom, God chose to introduce a new Christian practice to signify this New Covenant headship order. Although Christ became the Head of Man, Man remained the head of Woman, as he always had been. It is essential to understand that this New Covenant order, by which every believer is a priest to God, required new priestly dress code to reflect the changes in headship. Additionally, the New Covenant brought greater scriptural elevation and clarity of women's spiritual rights, which required visual signification to maintain spiritual order and prevent overextension or abuse of those new priestly rights. Therefore, headcovering serves as a reminder of the spiritual authorities and responsibilities that accompany this new order under the New Covenant.

If Paul anchors his reasoning for headcoverings in creation, did Eve wear a headcovering?

In a sinless state where perfect imaging and representation of divine order existed, it was unnecessary for Eve to wear a headcovering. Namely, there was no need for worship regulations as God was in perfect union with Adam and Eve. Furthermore, it is crucial to understand that Paul's basis for headcovering is rooted in creation principles, rather than creation practices. In a post-fall world, the practice of headcovering visually communicates a proper understanding of the biblical order of headship between men and women, which is based on the principles of God's design seen in the creation of Adam and Eve.

Peter talks about hair in his first epistle, so why doesn't he mention headcoverings?

In 1 Peter 3:3–4, the Apostle Peter emphasizes the importance of modesty among Christian women. He urges them to focus not on external adornments, such as braided hair, gold jewelry, or fine clothes, but rather on the inner person of the heart, characterized by a gentle and quiet spirit that is precious in God's sight. It is important to note that Peter is addressing a general ethic of modesty in daily life, rather than specific worship dress codes. His aim is to encourage women to value themselves based on how God sees them, rather than how they are perceived by others. The fact that Peter does not explicitly mention headcoverings in some of his writings does not necessarily mean that he rejected the practice. In 1 Corinthians 11:16, Paul refers to headcoverings as the practice of all the Apostles. Furthermore, historical records indicate that the doctrine of headcoverings was upheld by Linus, who was Peter's local successor. The *Liber Pontificalis*, an ancient Roman Catholic document, records that "He, by direction of the blessed Peter, decreed that a woman must veil her head to come into the church."[119]

---

119 Frederic P. Miller. Agnes F. Vandome, and John McBrewster, eds. 2010. Liber

I'm a pastor, and this book persuaded me. How should I implement this doctrine at our church?

As a pastor, it is important to communicate any shifts in doctrine clearly but implement them at the church gradually. One approach that has been successful is to start by walking out your convictions by having your wife wear her headcovering during worship. This will spark curiosity and conversations among the congregation, providing an opportunity to share your position and provide resources to help explain your interpretation of headcoverings. As the doctrine is discussed more, it will naturally lead to a time when the congregation can be properly guided through a series on headcoverings. Namely, unless you're already preaching through 1 Corinthians, pastors should avoid implementing this doctrine too quickly. Ultimately, it's important to exercise patience with your congregation and trust in the Lord's guidance, as He will work in His own time to bring His people along to this biblical position.

I used to belong to a church with legalistic and cult-like doctrine, and as a result, I associate headcoverings with that group. It's difficult for me to wear a headcovering again. What should I do?

First, let me express my condolences for the difficult experience you had with a group that distorted God's Word. I can relate, as I too left a legalistic church that did not understand the Gospel of grace. During that time, my wife started wearing a headcovering, but after we left the church and reevaluated everything,

---

Pontificalis. Alphascript Publishing.

we carefully examined what aligned with Scripture and what did not. Through this process, we realized that headcoverings, when understood in the context of the Gospel, can be a beautiful and significant practice. They are not intended to be a tool of oppression, but rather a way to honor the distinct roles of men and women, display our unique glories, express spiritual authority, and encourage worship. Despite any negative associations you may have with headcoverings, I encourage you not to let those experiences rob you of the beauty and truth of this practice. Rather, embrace it with joy, love, and reverence, and remember that it is not about fear or control, but about honoring God and His Word.

Section Four

CLOSING MATTERS

Appendix B

BLOCK DIAGRAM OF 1 CORINTHIANS 11:2–16

Block diagrams are a way for interpreters to lay out the text in main clauses (the underlined statements) and modifiers (the phrases placed below a word). This allows the interpreter to see more clearly how a particular phrase develops another clause or phrase. Visually, it allows you to see the biblical text in blocks instead of a paragraph format, which can make it more difficult to notice the author's intent.

The highlights in bold are certain types of clauses (causal clauses, contrast clauses, result clauses, purpose clauses, etc.). My purpose for showing this to you is to affirm to you that I am not projecting my opinions upon the text but extracting the meaning from the words of Scripture. Furthermore, you will notice that I have broken our text into several sections with their own heading to identify the function of each section.

Section #1: 11:2: A Praise for Obedience

2   Now
I praise you [main clause]
>   **because** you remember me [causal clause]
>>   in everything
>>   and
>>   hold firmly
>>>   to the traditions,
>>>   **just as** I delivered
them [contrast clause]
   to you.

Section #2: 11:3–6: An Argument from Authority

3   **But** [contrast clause]
I want you [main clause]
>   to understand
>>   that Christ is the head
>>>   of every man,
>>   and
>>   the man is the head
>>>   of a woman,
>>   and
>>   God is the head
>>>   of Christ.

APPENDIX B: BLOCK DIAGRAM   181

4 <u>Every man who has something</u> [main clause]
        on his head
            while praying
            or
            prophesying
                disgraces
                    his head.

5   **But** [contrast clause]
<u>every woman who has her head</u>
        uncovered
           while praying
           or
           prophesying
              disgraces
                her head,

for she is one [result clause]
    and
    the same
        as the woman [contrast clause]
            whose head
                is shaved.

6   **For if** a woman does not cover [result/contingency clause]
            her head,
<u>let her</u> also <u>have her hair cut off</u>;
  but [contrast clause]
    if it is disgraceful [contingency clause]
        for a woman

182 A COVER FOR GLORY

        to have her hair
             cut off
            or
        her head
             shaved,

<u>let her cover</u> [main clause]
    her head.

Section #3: 11:7–9: An Argument from Creation

7 **For** [result clause]
<u>a man ought not</u> [main clause]
    to have his head
        covered,
            since he is the image [causal clause]
                and
                glory
                  of God;
                      but the woman
[contrast clause]
is the glory
    of man.

8 **For** [result clause]
<u>man does not originate</u> [main clause]

>   from woman,
>
>   **but** [contrast clause]
>
>   woman
>
>   >   from man;

9   **for** indeed [causal clause]
<u>man was not created</u> [main clause]
>   >   for the woman's sake,
>   >
>   >   >   **but** woman [contrast clause]
>   >   >
>   >   >   >   for the man's sake.

Section #4: 11:10 An Argument from the Spiritual Realm

10   Therefore [result clause]
<u>the woman ought to have</u> [main clause]
>   >   a symbol
>   >
>   >   >   of authority
>   >   >
>   >   >   >   on her head,
>   >   >   >
>   >   >   >   >   **because** of the angels. [causal clause]

Section #5: 11:11–12: Men and Women Equal Before God

11   However,
>   in the Lord,

184 A COVER FOR GLORY

<u>neither is woman independent</u> [main clause]
>of man,
>>nor is man independent
>>>of woman.

12 **For** as [causal clause/contrast clause]
<u>the woman originates from the man,</u> [main clause]
>>so also [comparison clause]
>>the man
>>>has his birth
>>>>through the woman;
and
<u>all things originate</u> [main clause]
>from God.

Section #6: 11:13–15: An Argument from Nature

13 <u>Judge</u> [main clause]
>for yourselves:
>is it proper for a woman
>>to pray to God
>>>with her head
>>>>uncovered?

14 <u>Does not</u> even <u>nature</u> itself <u>teach you</u> [main clause]
>>that if a man

                        has long hair,
                                it is a dishonor
                                        to him,
15   but [contrast clause]
                                        if a woman has long hair,
                                                it is a glory
                                                        to her?
　For [causal clause]
her hair is given [main clause]
            to her
            for a covering.

Section #7: 11:16: An Argument from the Church

16　**But if** one [contrast/contingency clause]
                is inclined
                    to be contentious,
we have no other practice, [main clause]
                    nor have the churches
                                of God.

Closing Matters
SPECIAL THANKS

Though I have studied this doctrine off and on for nearly a decade prior to writing this book, my greatest resource was not found until my study commenced for this project. The book is titled *Good Order in the Church: The Head of Man is Christ, The Head of Woman is Man* by the late Dr. Leslie McFall. His 579-page masterpiece is, in my opinion, the world's leading work on the topic. You can find a free PDF of this work online.

All the great historical commentaries I leveraged from church history, including the works of Charles Hodge, John Calvin, Martin Luther, John Chrysostom, Tertullian, E.P. Gould, Joseph Agar Beet, Gordon H. Clark. John Gill, Matthew Henry, and several others.

Dr. Finny Kuruvilla produced a three-part video series available on YouTube titled *The Headcovering #1: Cultural or Counter-Cultural*. This resource was helpful, and I appreciated Dr. Kuruvilla's clear communication on this issue.

HeadcoveringMovement.org, which Jeremy Gardiner founded, was a useful archive of articles during my study.

Bnonn Tennant and Joel Webbon provided me with several strong resources.

David Phillips produced a useful Kindle book titled *Headcoverings Throughout Church History*.

Jess Hall, the President of Relearn Press, put extensive work into editing this manuscript.

Laramie Minga, our Theological Editor, reviewed and edited the manuscript for doctrinal integrity and clarity.

To the church ladies and elders from King's Way Bible Church who graciously read through the manuscript.

Closing Matters

BIBLIOGRAPHY

Ambrose, St. 2018. Exposition of the Christian Faith. Iv.28.32; Paradise Iv.24, x.28. Lighthouse Publishing.

Aquinas, Thomas. 2012. Commentary on the Letters of Saint Paul to the Corinthians (Latin-English Edition). Edited by The Aquinas Institute. Translated by Fabian R. Larcher. Aquinas Institute.

Augustine, St. 1979. In Ioannis Evangelium Tractatus 9, 10; Translated by W. A. Jurgens, The Faith of the Early Fathers. Vol. 3. Collegeville, MN: Liturgical Press.

Barrett, Michael P. V. 2003. Headcovering for Public Worship: An Exposition of 1 Corinthians 11:2–16. Greenville, CS: Faith Free Presbyterian Church. https://www.headcoveringmovement.com/Michael-Barrett-Head-Covering-for-Public-Worship.pdf.

Barth, Paul J. 2019. "Head Coverings in Worship?" Purely Presbyterian. July 15, 2019. https://purelypresbyterian.com/2019/07/15/head-coverings-in-worship/comment-page-1/.

Beet, Joseph Agar. 1882. A Commentary on St. Paul's Epistles to the Corinthians. London: Hodder and Stoughton.

Beza, Theodore. 1599. The New Testament of Our Lord Iesus Christ : Translated out of Greeke by Theod. Beza ; with Brief Summaries and Expositions upon the Hard Places by the Said Authour, Ioac. Camer., and P. Lofeler Villerius ; Englished by L. Tomson ; with Annotations of Fr. Iunius upon Revelation. London: Deputies of Christopher Barker.

Boekestein, William. n.d. "Six Benefits of Studying Church History." Reformation 21. Accessed February 2023. https://www.reformation21.org/blog/six-benefits-of-studying-church-history.

Brian Sauvé, Lexy Sauvé. 2023. Bright Hearth: What About Head Coverings? New Christendom Press. https://podcasts.apple.com/us/podcast/what-about-head-coverings/id1616730798?i=1000599283561.

Bridges, Jerry. 2017. Transforming Grace. Navpress Publishing Group.

Britannica, T. Editors of Encyclopaedia. 2008. "'Andania Mysteries.'" Encyclopedia Britannica. 2008. https://www.britannica.com/topic/Andania-mysteries.

Bushey, Scott. 2014. "What Does Church History Teach on Head Coverings? By Greg Price." Semperreformanda.com. Reformed Theology at Semper Reformanda. June 3, 2014. https://www.semperreformanda.com/the-regulative-principle-of-worship/the-regulative-principle-of-worship-articlesindex/what-does-church-history-teach-on-head-coverings-by-greg-price/.

Calvin, John. 2022. Commentary, Vol. 1: On the Epistles of Paul the Apostle to the Corinthians (Classic Reprint). London, England: Forgotten Books.

———. n.d. "Commentary on 1 Corinthians 11:2–16 Regarding Headcoverings." Covenanter.org. Accessed February 23, 2023. https://www.covenanter.org/reformed/2015/7/15/john-calvins-commentary-on-1-corinthians-112-16.

Chesterton, Gilbert Keith. 1994. Collected Works of G. K. Chesterton: Collected Poetry : Part 1 (Collected Works of Gk Chesterton). San Francisco, CA: Ignatius Press.

"Christian Head Covering." n.d. Wikipedia. Accessed March 18, 2023. https://en.wikipedia.org/wiki/Christian_head_covering.

Christianity Today. 1976. Vol. 20. Christianity Today.

Chrysostom, John. 2012. The Homilies of S. John Chrysostom, Archbishop of Constantinople on the First Epistle of St. Paul the Apostle to the Corinthians. Homily 26 on 1 Corinthians 11:2–16. General Books.

Clark, Gordon Haddon. 1991. First Corinthians: A Contemporary Commentary. 2nd ed. Trinity Foundation.

Clement of Alexandria. 2005. "The Instructor. Book III Chapter XI." Early Christian Writings. 2005. http://www.earlychristianwritings.com/text/clement-instructor-book3.html.

Colet, John. 2012. An Exposition of St. Paul's First Epistle to the Corinthians. General Books.

Cotton, John. (1642) 2008. The True Constitution of a Particular Visible

Church. Shropshire, England: Quinta Press.

Crichton, Michael. n.d. "Michael Crichton Quotes." Goodreads.com. Accessed February 23, 2023. https://www.goodreads.com/quotes/188569-if-you-don-t-know-history-then-you-don-t-know-anything.

Derrett, J. Duncan M. 1977. Studies in the New Testament, Volume 1 Glimpses of the Legal and Social Presuppositions of the Authors. Article: Religious Hair. Leiden, Netherlands: Brill.

Dodson, James. 2016. "The Public Preaching of Women. — Reformed Presbyterian Church (Covenanted) - 'Steelite' Covenanters." Reformed Presbyterian Church (Covenanted) - "Steelite"Covenanters. May 24, 2016. https://www.covenanter.org/reformed/2016/5/22/the-public-preaching-of-women.

Durandus, Gulielmus. 2008. The Rationale Divinorum Officiorum: The Foundational Symbolism of the Early Church, Its Structure, Decoration, Sacraments, and Vestments. Louisville, KY: Fons Vitae.

Edwards, John. (1692) 2011. An Enquiry into Four Remarkable Texts of the New Testament Which Contain Some Difficulty in Them, with a Probable Resolution of Them. Proquest, Eebo Editions.

"Elizabeth Farians: Catholic Feminist Pioneer." n.d. Feminist Studies in Religion. Accessed February 23, 2023. https://www.fsrinc.org/elizabeth-farians/.

Elliot, Elisabeth. 2021. Recovering Biblical Manhood and Womanhood: A Response to Evangelical Feminism (Chapter: The Essence of Femininity: A Personal Perspective). Edited by John Piper and Wayne Grudem. Wheaton, IL: Crossway Books.

Ellison, Renee. 2022. The Biblical Headcovering: Scarf of Hidden Power. Arizona: Independent Publishing.

Evans, Rachel Held. 2012. "For the Sake of the Gospel, Let Women Speak." Rachel Held Evans. June 7, 2012. https://rachelheldevans.com/blog/mutuality-let-women-speak.

Fabry, Merrill. 2016. "Now You Know: How Did Long Hair Become a Thing for Women?" Time, June 16, 2016. https://time.com/4348252/history-long-hair/.

Findlayson, Rev Bryan. n.d. "Exegetical Commentary on 1 Corinthians 11:2–16." Lectionarystudies.com. Christian Ministry Resources. Accessed February 23, 2023. http://www.lectionarystudies.com/studyn/epiphany1epfen.html.

Finnegan, Leah. 2017. "When Men Fear Women." The Outline. October 24, 2017. https://theoutline.com/post/2421/when-men-fear-women.

G., Jeremy. 2017. "Can Wedding Rings Replace Head Covering?" The Head Covering Movement. March 28, 2017. https://www.headcoveringmovement.com/articles/can-wedding-rings-replace-head-covering.

Gardina Pestana, Carla. 2004. Quakers and Baptists in Colonial Massachusetts. Cambridge, England: Cambridge University Press.

Gardiner, Jeremy. 2017. "Can Wedding Rings Replace Head Covering?" The Head Covering Movement. March 28, 2017. https://www.headcoveringmovement.com/articles/can-wedding-rings-replace-head-covering.

Gill, John. 1746. "Gill's Exposition of the Entire Bible. Commentary on

1 Corinthians 11 . 1999." Study Light. 1746. https://www.studylight.org/commentaries/eng/geb/1-corinthians-11.html.

Gryboski, Michael. 2021. "Women's History Month: 7 Christian Denominations That Voted to Allow Female Ordination." The Christian Post. March 7, 2021. https://www.christianpost.com/news/7-christian-denominations-that-allow-women-to-be-ordained.html.

Halicarnassensis, Dionysius. 1758. The Roman Antiquities. United Kingdom: University of Lausanne.

Henry, Carl, ed. 1986. Biblical Expositor: The Living Theme of the Great Book-3 Vols. Baker Publishing Group.

Hodge, Charles. 1974. Commentary on Corinthians I and II. Edinburgh, Scotland: Banner of Truth Trust.

Holmes, Tao Tao. 2016. "When Going out without a Hat Was Grounds for Scandal." Atlas Obscura. March 21, 2016. https://www.atlasobscura.com/articles/when-going-out-without-a-hat-was-grounds-for-scandal.

Ignatius, Mar David. n.d. "Bishop's Epistle." Blogspot.com. Accessed February 23, 2023. http://bishopjerrylhayes.blogspot.com/2020/07/in-quote-from-modern-cinema-particular.html.

Joel Webbon, Bnonn Tennant. 2022. Biblical Womanhood & Head Coverings Joel Webbon and Bnonn Tennant. Texas: Right Response Ministries.

Kassian, Mary A. 2000. The Feminist Mistake: The Radical Impact of Feminism on Church and Culture. Wheaton, IL: Crossway Books.
Kayser, Phillip. 2018. Glory and Covering: A Study of 1 Corinthians 11:1–16.

United States: Biblical Blueprints.

Kittel, G., and Gerhard Friedrich, eds. 1959. Theological Dictionary of the New Testament. Translated by Geoffrey W. Bromiley. Grand Rapids, MI: William B Eerdmans Publishing.

Knight, G. W. 1979. The Role Relation of Man and Woman and the Teaching/Ruling Functions in the Church. Chicago, IL: Journal of Evangelical Theological Society. https://www.etsjets.org/files/JETS-PDFs/18/18-2/18-2-pp081-091_JETS.pdf.

Knight, Robert. 1849. Rebuke of Women Praying with Uncovered Heads: A New Interpretation of 1 Corinthians. Journal of Sacred Literature 4.

Knox, John. 1986. The Political Writings: First Blast of the Trumpet against the Monstrous Regiment of Women and Other Selected Works. Cranbury, NJ: Folger Books.

Kuruvilla, Finny. 2018. The Headcovering #1: Cultural or Counter-Cultural. United States: YouTube. https://www.youtube.com/watch?v=QA-4bxP0nY_0.

Leap, Dennis. n.d. "How Feminism Harms Families." Thetrumpet.com. Accessed February 23, 2023. https://www.thetrumpet.com/2384-how-feminism-harms-families.

MacArthur, John. 2023. "Head Coverings for Women." Grace to You. January 24, 2023. https://www.gty.org/library/bibleqnas-library/QA0219/head-coverings-for-women.

Mansi, Giovan Domenico, Philippe Labbe, and Jean Baptiste Martin. 2019.

Sacrorum Conciliorum Nova Et Amplissima Collectio, Cujus Johannes Dominicus Mansi Et Post Ipsius Mortem Florentius Et Venetianus Editores AB Anno 1758 Ad Annum 1798 Priores Triginta Unum Tomos Ediderunt, Nunc Autem Continuatat Et Absoluta, Volume 33. Wentworth Press.

Marlowe, Michael. 2005. "Headcoverings in the Ancient World." Bible Researcher. 2005. http://www.bible-researcher.com/headcoverings3.html.

McFall, Leslie. 2002. Good Order in the Church: The Head of Man Is Christ, The Head of Woman Is Man. England: Self-Published.

Melanchthon, Philipp. 2011. The Augsburg Confession: Article 28:54–55. Tredition Classics.

Merry Wiesner-Hanks, Susan Karant-Nunn. 2012. Luther on Women: A Sourcebook. Cambridge, UK20: Cambridge University Press.

Miller, Frederic P., Agnes F. Vandome, and John McBrewster, eds. 2010. Liber Pontificalis. Alphascript Publishing.

Mouser, Bill. 2007. "Hair and Worship." Archive.org. 2007. https://web.archive.org/web/20150715060616/http://fiveaspects.net/hair-and-worship/.

Oakes, Anna. 2020. "Amid Growth in Leadership, One-Fifth of U.S. Clergy Are Female." Watauga Democrat. March 1, 2020. https://www.wataugademocrat.com/community/amid-growth-in-leadership-one-fifth-of-u-s-clergy-are-female/article_739b14a1-212a-5d06-b429-4d888a369255.html.

Oster, Richard. 1988. When Men Wore Veils to Worship: The Historical Context of 1 Corinthians 11.4. New Testament Studies 34, No. 4. Cambridge,

UK: Cambridge University Press.

Parsons, Sister Wilfrid. 1956. Letters, Volume 5 (204–270) (The Fathers of the Church, Volume 32). Catholic University of America Press.

Phillips, David. 2014. Headcovering Throughout Christian History: The Church's Response to 1 Corinthians 11:2–16 (Covered Glory). Self-Published.

Plutarch. 1874. Plutarch's Morals Translated from the Greek by Several Hands. Corrected and Revised by. William W. Goodwin, PH. D. Boston. Little, Brown, and Company. Cambridge: UK: Cambridge Press Of John Wilson and Son.

———. 2013. Romane Questions. United States: Rarebooksclub.com.

———. 2018. Sayings of the Spartans. Translated by Frank Cole Babbit. Vol. 3. Vigeo Press.

Richardson, Ernest Cushing, Bernhard Pick, and James Donaldson. 2015. The Ante-Nicene Fathers. Translations of the Writings of the Fathers down to A.d. 325 Volume 7, Book II, Section VII, On Assembling in the Church. Arkose Press.

Roberts, Alexander, ed. 2007. The Ante-Nicene Fathers: The Writings of the Fathers down to A.d. 325 Volume IV Fathers of the Third Century -Tertullian Part 4; Minucius Felix. New York, NY: Cosimo Classics.

Robertson, A. T. 1982. Word Pictures in the New Testament. 1 Corinthians, Vol. 1 11:15. Ada, OK: Revell.

Schaff, Philip, ed. 2007. Nicene and Post-Nicene Fathers: Second Series,

Volume VI Jerome: Letters and Select Works. New York, NY: Cosimo Classics.

———. 2010. Ante-Nicene Fathers, Volume 3. Grand Rapids, MI: Christian Classics Ethereal Library.

———. 2012. History of the Christian Church, Volume 8 Modern Christianity the Swiss Reformation. Rarebooksclub.com.

———. (1887) 2012. Nicene and Post-Nicene Fathers. Vol. 3. Buffalo, NY: Christian Literature Publishing Co.

———. 2017. Ante-Nicene Fathers: Volume II. Fathers of the Second Century: Tatian, Theophilus of Antioch, Athenagoras of Athens, Clement of Alexandria. Two, Book Five, The Instructor, Book 3, Chapter 11. Edited by Alexander Roberts and James Donaldson. Grand Rapids, MI: Christian Classics Ethereal Library.

Schmidt, Alvin J., ed. 1880. The Liturgy and Ritual of the Celtic Church. Vol. 10. The Church Quarterly Review.

———. 1991. Veiled and Silenced: How Culture Shaped Sexist Theology. Mercer University Press.

Shapouri, Beth. 2011. "Want to Know What Men Really Notice When It Comes to Your Hair? Check out These Survey Results." Glamour. February 9, 2011. https://www.glamour.com/story/want-to-know-what-men-really-n.

Signori, Gabriela. 2005. Reflections on an Asymmetrical Relationship in The Medieval History Journal. London : Sage Publications.
Simms, Luma. 2013. "Uncovering the Head Covering Debate." CT Women.

October 1, 2013. https://www.christianitytoday.com/ct/2013/october-web-only/uncovering-head-covering-debate.html.

Skolnitsky, John Calvin Seth. 1992. Sermon on 1 Cor 11:2–3. Philidelphia, PA: Presbyterian Heritage Publications.

Sproul, R. C. 2016. Knowing Scripture. Downers Grove, IL: Inter-Varsity Press.

———. 2021. Essential Truths of Christian Faith. Wheaton, IL: Tyndale House.

———. n.d. "To Cover or Not to Cover." Ligonier. Accessed February 2023a. https://www.ligonier.org/learn/series/hard-sayings-of-the-apostles/to-cover-or-not-to-cover.

———. n.d. "To Cover or Not to Cover." Ligonier. Accessed March 18, 2023b. www.ligonier.org/learn/series/hard_sayings_of_the_apostles/to-cover-or-not-to-cover/.

Spurgeon, C. H. 1996. Spurgeon's Sermons on Angels. Grand Rapids, MI: Kregel Publications.

Spurgeon, Charles H. 2022. Commenting & Commentaries. Legare Street Press.

Stenn, Kurt S. 2017. Hair - A Human History. New York, NY: Pegasus Books.

Tamás Bereczkei, Norbert Meskó. 2006. "Hair Length, Facial Attractiveness, Personality Attribution: A Multiple Fitness Model of Hairdressing." https://www.researchgate.net/publication/235933312_Hair_length_facial_

attractiveness_personality_attribution_A_multiple_fitness_model_of_hair-dressing.

Tennant, Dominic Bnonn. 2019. "Head Coverings #1: The Logic of Glory and Veiling Bnonn Tennant." Bnonn Tennant (blog). Information Highwayman. August 23, 2019. https://bnonn.com/head-coverings-1/.

Tertullian. 2018. A Treatise on the Soul. Lighthouse Publishing.

———. n.d. "On the Veiling of Virgins: Chapter 1. Truth Rather to Be Appealed to Than Custom, and Truth Progressive in Its Developments." New Advent. https://www.newadvent.org/fathers/0403.htm.

The Westminster Larger Catechism: Extended Annotated Edition. Question 178: What Is Prayer? 2012. Altenmünster, Germany: Jazzybee Verlag.

Toynbee, Arnold. 1969. Crucible of Christianity. London, England: Thames & Hudson.

United States Congress House, and Strabo. 2013. Strabonis Geographica. Rarebooksclub.com.

Waltke, Bruce. 1992. "The Role of Women in Worship in the Old Testament." Ldolphin.org. 1992. http://www.ldolphin.org/waltke.html.

Waltke, Bruce K., ed. 1978. 1 Corinthians 11:2–16: An Interpretation by Bruce K. Waltke. Vol. BSAC 135. Bibliotheca Sacra. https://www.scribd.com/document/220628251/Waltke-1Corinthians-11-2-16-an-Interpretation.

Warren, F. E., and Jane Stevenson. 1987. Liturgy and Ritual of the Celtic

Church. Woodbridge, England: Boydell Press.

Wesley, John. 1990. Wesley's Notes on the Bible. Grand Rapids, MI: Zondervan.

"What Americans Think about Women in Power." n.d. Barna Group. Accessed February 23, 2023. https://www.barna.com/research/americans-think-women-power/.

Wikipedia contributors. n.d. "Las Sinsombrero." Wikipedia, The Free Encyclopedia. https://es.wikipedia.org/w/index.php?title=Las_Sinsombrero&oldid=149441201.

Witherington, Ben. 1995. Conflict and Community in Corinth: A Socio-Rhetorical Commentary on 1 and 2 Corinthians. Grand Rapids, MI: William B Eerdmans Publishing.

Zuck, Roy B. 2013. Basic Bible Interpretation. Colorado Springs, CO: David C Cook Publishing Company.

Shop.Relearn.org

OTHER TITLES BY DALE PARTRIDGE

LEARN BIBLICAL MANHOOD

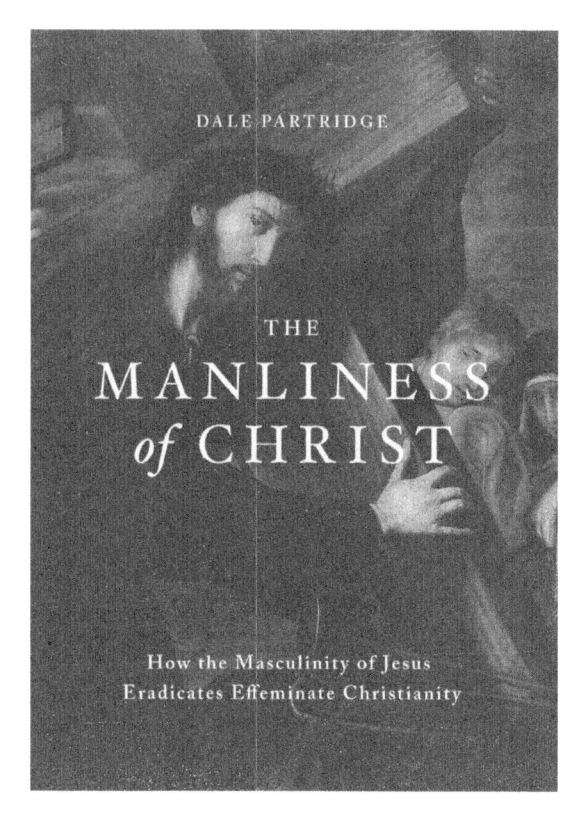

DALE PARTRIDGE

THE
MANLINESS
of CHRIST

How the Masculinity of Jesus
Eradicates Effeminate Christianity

Relearn.org/Man

AN INTRODUCTION TO THEOLOGY

Relearn.org/Theology

AFFIRM YOUR CHILD'S GOD-GIVEN GENDER

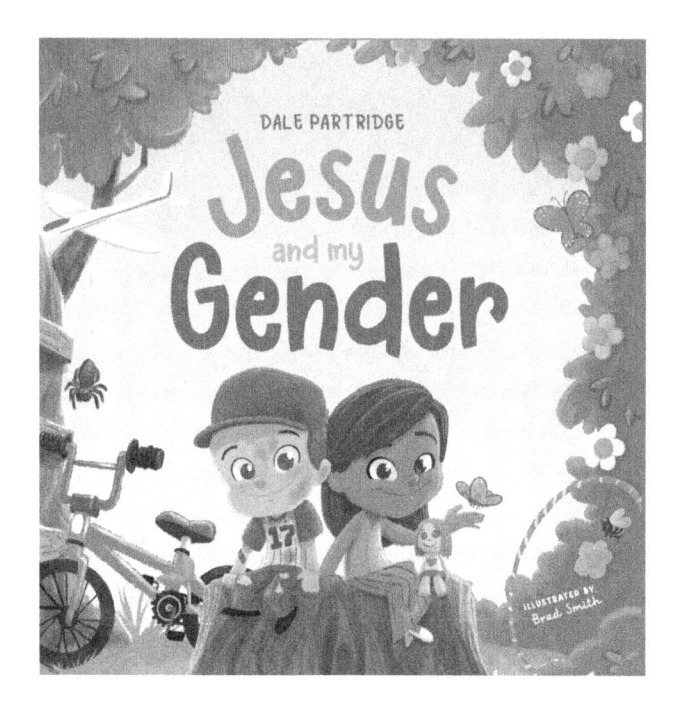

Relearn.org/Gender

READ THE GOSPEL

A Simple Presentation of

THE
GOSPEL

A MESSAGE *of* LOVE

FINDING FORGIVENESS, FREEDOM, & FAMILY

MailtheGospel.org

Made in the USA
Middletown, DE
14 April 2023